# SMP 11-16

# Book R3

CAMBRIDGE
UNIVERSITY PRESS

Published by the Press Syndicate of the University of Cambridge
The Pitt Building, Trumpington Street, Cambridge CB2 1RP
40 West 20th Street, New York, NY 10011–4211, USA
10 Stamford Road, Oakleigh, Victoria 3166, Australia

First published 1987
Fifth printing 1992

Illustrations by Chris Evans and David Parkins
Diagrams and phototypesetting by Parkway Group, London and
Abingdon, and Gecko Limited, Bicester, Oxon.
Photographs by John Ling
Cover photograph of Romanian panpipes (*nai*) circa 1950 from the Horniman
Museum, London, by Nigel Luckhurst.

Printed in Great Britain by Scotprint, Musselburgh, Scotland

*British Library cataloguing in publication data*
SMP 11–16 red series.
Bk R3
1. Mathematics – 1961–
I. School Mathematics Project
510      QA39.2
ISBN 0 521 31456 9

**Acknowledgements**
The authors and the publisher would like to thank the following
for permission to reproduce copyright material: Oxford and
Cambridge Schools Examination Board and the East Anglian
Examinations Board question B1, page 13); *The Times*
(page 75); Thomas Cook (page 118).

# Contents

# 1 Trigonometry (1)

## A  Sides and angles in a right-angled triangle

The word 'trigonometry' comes from Greek words meaning 'triangle measurement'. In trigonometry we study the relationships between the sides and angles of right-angled triangles. First you need to know some words which are used to describe the sides of a triangle.

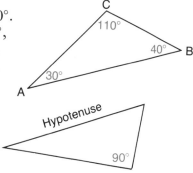

Here is a triangle ABC, whose angles are 30°, 40° and 110°.
In this triangle, the side AB is **opposite** the angle of 110°,
            the side BC is **opposite** the angle of 30°,
            the side AC is **opposite** the angle of 40°.

In a right-angled triangle, the longest side is always opposite the right-angle, and is called the **hypotenuse**.

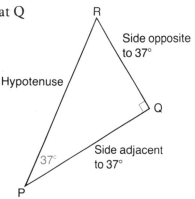

Here is a right-angled triangle PQR. The right-angle is at Q and the angle at P is 37°.

The side PR is the **hypotenuse**.
The side QR is **opposite** the angle of 37°.
We say the side PQ is **adjacent** to the angle of 37°.

('Adjacent' means 'next to'. There are in fact two sides which are next to the angle of 37°, PQ and PR.
But PR already has the special name hypotenuse, so only PQ is called the side adjacent to 37°.)

A1  For each of these right-angled triangles, write down which side is
(i) the hypotenuse  (ii) opposite angle $a$  (iii) adjacent to angle $a$

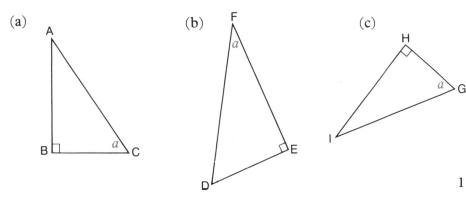

(a)

(b)

(c)

## B Similar right-angled triangles

These are all right-angled triangles. Every one has an angle of 35° in it.

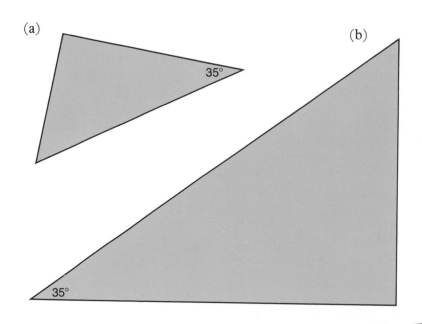

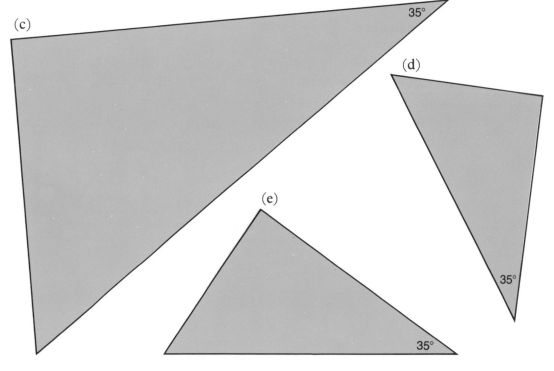

The triangles on the opposite page are all **similar** to each other. You can see this when they are cut out and placed on top of one another.

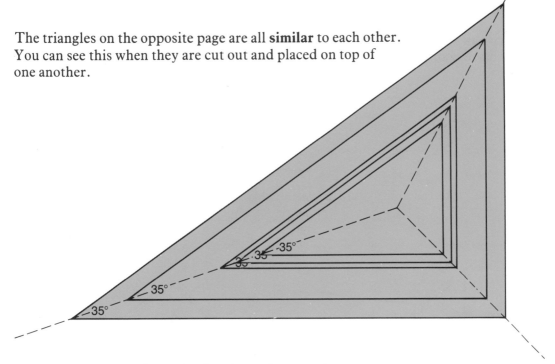

**B1** Do this for each triangle on the opposite page:
  (i) Measure the side opposite 35°.
  (ii) Measure the side adjacent to 35°.
  (iii) Calculate the ratio $\dfrac{\text{side opposite } 35°}{\text{side adjacent to } 35°}$, to 1 decimal place.

In any right-angled triangle with an angle of 35° in it, the ratio $\dfrac{\text{side opposite } 35°}{\text{side adjacent to } 35°}$ is 0·7.

35°
Side adjacent to 35°
Side opposite 35°

So the side opposite 35° is 0·7 times the side adjacent to 35°.

35°
×0·7
Side adjacent to 35°
Side opposite 35°

You can use this fact to calculate the side opposite 35° when you know the side adjacent to 35°.

For example, when the side adjacent to 35° is 4 cm, the side opposite 35° is 4 cm × 0·7 = **2·8 cm**.

35° ×0·7
4 cm
2·8 cm

**B2** Calculate the side opposite 35° in this triangle.

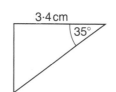
3·4 cm
35°

3

The triangles drawn in red on this picture are all right-angled triangles.
Every one has an angle of 35° in it.

**B3** Calculate the heights marked $a$, $b$, $c$ in these diagrams.

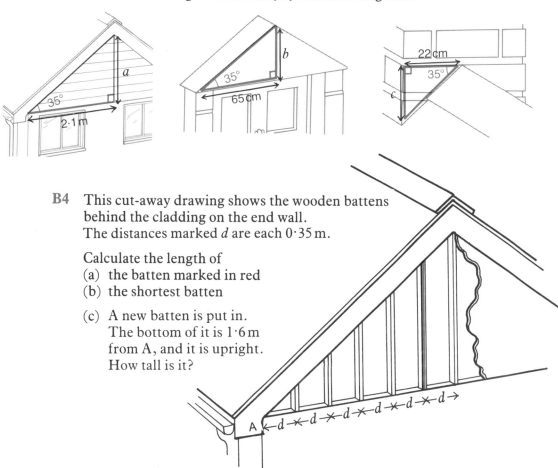

**B4** This cut-away drawing shows the wooden battens
behind the cladding on the end wall.
The distances marked $d$ are each $0 \cdot 35$ m.

Calculate the length of
(a) the batten marked in red
(b) the shortest batten

(c) A new batten is put in.
The bottom of it is $1 \cdot 6$ m
from A, and it is upright.
How tall is it?

**B5** A TV aerial is erected by the
dormer window. The pole is
$2 \cdot 1$ m long. What length of pole
is above the roof of the window?

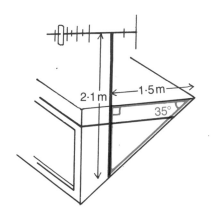

**B6** The ladder reaches $4 \cdot 6$ m up the
wall. How far is the bottom of the
ladder from the wall?

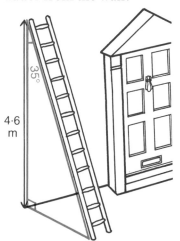

## C  The tangent of an angle

In a right-angled triangle with an angle of 35°

in it, the ratio $\dfrac{\text{side opposite } 35°}{\text{side adjacent to } 35°}$ is 0·7.

(To 7 decimal places, the ratio is 0·700 207 5.)

The ratio is called the **tangent of 35°**.

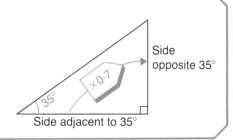

Side opposite 35°

Side adjacent to 35°

The ratio has a different value when the angle is different.

For example, in a right-angled triangle with

an angle of 50° in it, the ratio $\dfrac{\text{side opposite } 50°}{\text{side adjacent to } 50°}$

is 1·191 753 6 (to 7 decimal places).

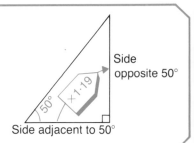

Side opposite 50°

Side adjacent to 50°

Here is a table of some angles and their tangents. Each tangent is given correct to 3 decimal places.

| Angle | 0° | 5° | 10° | 15° | 20° | 25° | 30° | 35° | 40° |
|---|---|---|---|---|---|---|---|---|---|
| **Tangent** | 0 | 0·087 | 0·176 | 0·268 | 0·364 | 0·466 | 0·577 | 0·700 | 0·839 |

| Angle | 45° | 50° | 55° | 60° | 65° | 70° | 75° | 80° | 85° |
|---|---|---|---|---|---|---|---|---|---|
| **Tangent** | 1 | 1·192 | 1·428 | 1·732 | 2·145 | 2·747 | 3·732 | 5·671 | 11·430 |

The Greek letter $\theta$ ('theta') is often used to stand for an angle.
In a right-angled triangle with an angle $\theta$ in it,

the ratio $\dfrac{\text{side opposite } \theta}{\text{side adjacent to } \theta}$ is the tangent of $\theta$ (written **tan $\theta$** for short).

This diagram shows that you calculate the side opposite $\theta$ by
multiplying the side adjacent to $\theta$ by tan $\theta$.

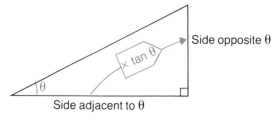

Side opposite $\theta$

Side adjacent to $\theta$

Side adjacent to $\theta$ × tan $\theta$ = side opposite $\theta$

You may find it helpful to copy this diagram and the formula
into your book.

## Worked example

Calculate the side opposite 20° in this triangle.

The angle of 20° is at the top of the triangle. The side adjacent to 20° is 4·6 m long.

So 4·6 m × tan 20° = side opposite 20°.

From the table of tangents, tan 20° = 0·364, so the side opposite 20° = 4·6 m × 0·364
= **1·7 m** (to 1 d.p.).

**C1**   Calculate the lengths marked with letters in these diagrams.
Give each answer correct to the nearest 0·1 m.

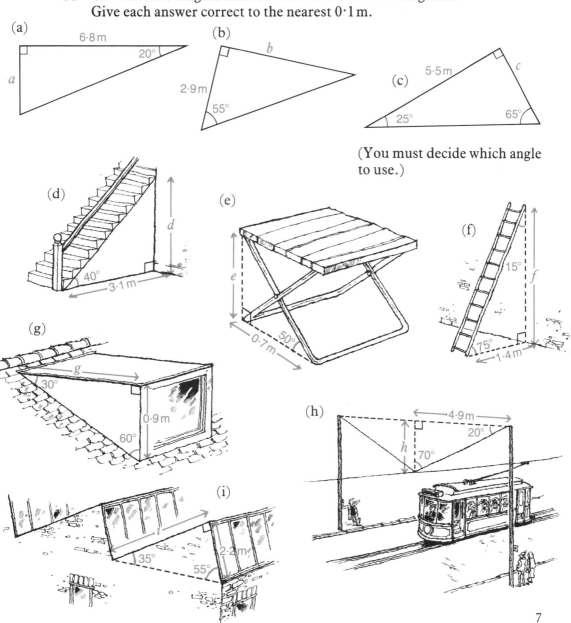

(a)   6·8 m   20°   a

(b)   b   2·9 m   55°

(c)   5·5 m   c   25°   65°

(You must decide which angle to use.)

(d)   d   40°   3·1 m

(e)   e   0·7 m   50°

(f)   15°   f   75°   1·4 m

(g)   g   30°   0·9 m   60°

(h)   4·9 m   20°   h   70°

(i)   i   35°   2·1 m   55°

7

## D Using a calculator

On a scientific calculator you will find a key marked tan .
Before you use it, make sure the calculator is set to work in degrees.

To find tan 25°, first enter 25 and then press tan .
The calculator will give the result 0·466 307 . . . depending on how
many figures it displays.

> **D1** Use a calculator to find these.
>     (a) tan 37°    (b) tan 53°    (c) tan 22·5°    (d) tan 89·9°

You can use a calculator to work out the side opposite a given angle
in a right-angled triangle, when you know the side adjacent to the angle.
In the triangle on the right,

$$5·7\,m \times \tan 23° = AB.$$

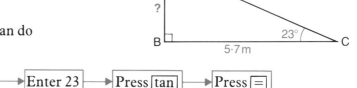

On most calculators you can do
5·7 × tan 23° like this:

Enter 5·7 ⟶ Press ☓ ⟶ Enter 23 ⟶ Press tan ⟶ Press =

The result should be 2·419 506 . . . So AB = 2·4 m to 1 d.p.

> **D2** Calculate, correct to 1 d.p.,    (a) 4·6 × tan 54°    (b) 72·3 × tan 9°

> **D3** Calculate the sides marked with letters, to the nearest 0·1 m.

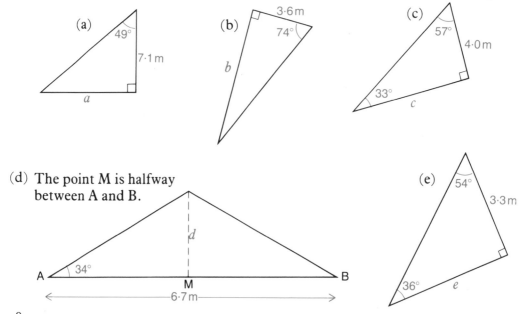

8

**D4**  This diagram shows the
cross-section of a railway
embankment.

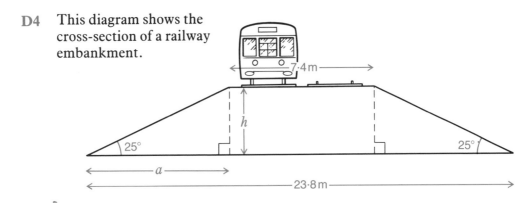

(a) Calculate the length marked *a* in the diagram.

(b) Calculate the height marked *h*.

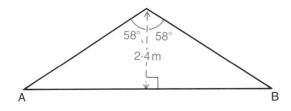

**D5**  Calculate the length AB in the
diagram on the left.

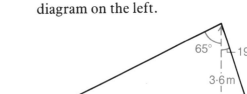

**D6**  Calculate CD in the diagram
on the right. (Split CD into
two parts.)

## Angles of elevation

If you stand and look directly at the top of a tall tree,
your line of sight slopes upwards from the horizontal.
The angle between your line of sight and the horizontal
is called the **angle of elevation** of the top of the tree from
where you are standing.

Surveyors measure angles of elevation with an
instrument called a 'theodolite'.

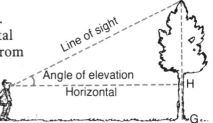

**D7**  Suppose that the distance MH in the picture is 10 metres,
and the angle of elevation is 25°.
(a) Calculate the distance TH, to the nearest 0·1 metre.
(b) To find the height of the tree, you have to add the distance HG.
This is the same as the height of the man's eyes above the ground.
If his eyes are 1·6 m above the ground, how high is the tree?

**D8**  The same man stands 25 m away from a flagpole and finds that the
angle of elevation of the top of the pole is 41°. How tall is the pole?

9

# 2 Arranging and selecting (1)

## A  Timetables

Young people come to an adventure holiday centre for five days.
The warden divides them into three groups, A, B and C.
There are five activities, and each group does a different one each day.

Water safety

Map reading
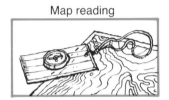

Hill walking

Canoeing

Athletics

The warden makes a chart like this. He has filled in the week's activities
for one of the groups.

|          | Monday      | Tuesday      | Wednesday | Thursday     | Friday    |
|----------|-------------|--------------|-----------|--------------|-----------|
| Group A  | Map reading | Water safety | Canoeing  | Hill walking | Athletics |
| Group B  |             |              |           |              |           |
| Group C  |             |              |           |              |           |

There are three rules for planning the activities:

- Every group must do water safety before it does canoeing.
- Every group must do map reading before it does hill walking.
- Two or more groups cannot be doing the same activity on the same day.

**A1**  Copy the warden's chart. Put in the activities he has planned
for group A. Check that they obey the first two rules.

Now complete the chart for the other groups, making sure that
you obey all three rules.
You may have to try different arrangements before you find one
that obeys all the rules. So work in pencil, or cut out pieces of
paper with the activities written on them and move them around
on your chart until you have a plan that works.

**A2** Five students, Rachel, Sadia, Kevin, Martin and Peter, go on a five-day craft course. Each student has to spend three of the days in the pottery. There is room in the pottery for only three students at a time.

Copy this chart. Rachel's days in the pottery are already filled in.

Complete the chart.

| | Day 1 | 2 | 3 | 4 | 5 |
|---|---|---|---|---|---|
| Rachel | ✓ | ✓ | | | ✓ |
| Sadia | | | | | |
| Kevin | | | | | |
| Martin | | | | | |
| Peter | | | | | |

**A3** Four people work in an office. Each one gets 3 weeks' holiday, but not more than 2 weeks can be taken in any one stretch.

They all have to take their holidays within a period of 6 weeks, but not more than two of them are allowed to be away at the same time.

(a) Two people, Janet and Rajesh, have already fixed up their holidays, as in this chart.

| | Week 1 | Week 2 | Week 3 | Week 4 | Week 5 | Week 6 |
|---|---|---|---|---|---|---|
| Janet | ✓ | ✓ | | ✓ | | |
| Rajesh | ✓ | ✓ | | | | ✓ |
| Patrick | | | | | | |
| Gillian | | | | | | |

Can the other two people arrange their holidays without breaking the rules? If so, show how it can be done.

(b) If Rajesh moves his one week from week 6 to week 5, can Patrick and Gillian arrange their holidays without breaking the rules? If so, show how it can be done.

**A4** Five basketball teams, A, B, C, D and E, decide to have a tournament. Each team has to play every other team once. Each team has to have at least one game's rest between playing.

For example, they might start like this:

| 1st game | 2nd game | 3rd game |
|---|---|---|
| A plays B. C, D and E rest. | C plays D. A, B and E rest. | . . . . . . |

Make a chart like this and use it to plan the tournament. (You do not have to start with teams playing as shown here.)

When you think you have finished, check that each team has played every other team.

A5 In the office at Mayhem's stores, everybody gets a fortnight's holiday.

(People are not allowed to take two separate weeks.)

The store manager gets first choice.
If the store manager is away, her secretary must be present.
If the chief buyer is away, his secretary must be present.
The two secretaries cannot be away at the same time.

The chief cashier is married to the transport supervisor, so they always take their holidays together.

There must be at least four people present at any time.

In the office there is a chart for planning holidays.

There are six pieces of grey card which can be moved around.

Each piece represents someone's holiday.

**Summer Holiday Planner** ☼

| Week no. | 1 | 2 | 3 | 4 | 5 | 6 | 7 | 8 |
|---|---|---|---|---|---|---|---|---|
| Store manager | | ▓ | ▓ | | | | | |
| Store manager's secretary | | | | ▓ | ▓ | | | |
| Chief cashier | ▓ | ▓ | | | | | | |
| Chief buyer | | | | | | | ▓ | ▓ |
| Chief buyer's secretary | | | | | ▓ | ▓ | | |
| Transport supervisor | ▓ | ▓ | | | | | | |

(a) There are three things wrong with the holiday plan shown. What are they?

(b) Copy the planner on squared paper, without the grey pieces.
Cut out the six pieces from paper or card.
Try to make a holiday plan by moving the pieces around, but keep the store manager's holiday in weeks 2 and 3.

When you think you have a plan which does not break any of the rules, ask someone to check it. Then shade where the pieces go.

(c) It is possible to squeeze all the holidays into only 7 weeks instead of 8? Does the store manager have to change her weeks?

(d) Is it possible to squeeze them all into 6 weeks?

12

**A6** The full-time staff of a sports centre are

the manager,　the caretaker,　two clerical staff,　two instructors.

Make an 8-week holiday plan for them, following these rules:

Everybody gets a fortnight's holiday (two weeks together), except the caretaker; he gets three weeks off and insists on having weeks 2, 3 and 4.

There must not be more than two people off at any one time.

The clerical staff cannot be off together.

The instructors cannot be off together.

If the caretaker is off, there must be two instructors present.

**A7** Can the holidays in question A6 be squeezed into 7 weeks?

# B Seating arrangements

**B1** On a school coach trip, five boys, Adam, Bob, Charlie, David and Edward, plan to travel on the back seat.

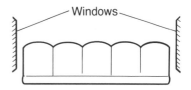

Adam and Bob always sit together.

Charlie and David often fight, so there must be at least two people between them.

Edward cannot sit next to a window because it makes him sick.

List all the possible arrangements in which the five boys can sit. (Use A for Adam, B for Bob, etc.)

**B2** There are six people: A, B, C, D, E and F.

Not everyone knows everyone else. These pairs know each other:

| | | | |
|---|---|---|---|
| A and B | A and C | A and D | A and E |
| A and F | B and D | C and E | D and F |

The six people have to sit in a row, so that nobody is next to a person they don't know.

Find a way to seat them. How many different ways can you find?

The problem in question B2 is easier to solve if you use a **network** to represent the information about which people know each other.

A network is simply a collection of dots with lines joining some or all of the pairs of dots.

**1** Represent each person by a dot.

Whenever two people know one another, join their two dots.

For example, A and F know one another.

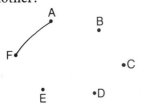

**2** Here is the complete network.

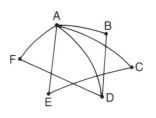

**3** Try starting with A.
A knows B, so we could put B next, . . .

. . . and B knows D, so D could come next, . . .

. . . and D knows F, . . .

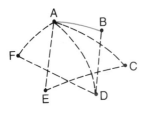

**4** But then who? The only other line from F returns to A, so there is nobody left who can sit next to F!

What we need is a **tour** – a route through the network which visits every dot just once.

**5** For example, we could go CEAFDB, or in reverse order BDFAEC.
These are not the only solutions. Counting reversals there are 8 solutions altogether.

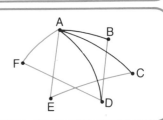

**B3** Copy the network. Find as many as you can of the other 6 solutions to the puzzle.
Write down the sequence of letters in each case.

B4　There are five people: A, B, C, D and E.
These pairs know one another: A, C　A, D　B, C　C, D　D, E

(a) Draw a network to represent this information.

(b) Find a way to stand the five people in a line so that nobody is next to a stranger.

(c) How many different ways are there to do it?

(d) Which two people must stand at the ends of the line?

(e) The five people are joined by an extra person F who knows only A. In how many ways can all six people stand in line with nobody next to a stranger? Explain your answer.

B5　Two words are 'friendly' if they have only one letter different. For example, SOUR is friendly with HOUR, SPUR, SOAR, SOUL, etc.

In a 'word chain' each word is friendly with the next. For example, here is how to change BEER into WINE:

BEER　　BEET　　BENT　　WENT　　WANT　　WANE　　WINE

A closed chain is also possible. For example,

PLOT
SLOT
PLOP
SLOP

(a) Draw a network with eight dots for these words:
FLAT　SLAG　SLIT　SLAB　FLAB　SLAT　FLAG　FLIT

Connect the dots whenever two words are friendly.

(b) Find two different ways to connect the words in a closed chain.

B6　Seven people, A, B, C, D, E, F and G are going for a meal together. They have to sit round a circular table.

The following pairs know one another.

| A, B | A, C | A, D | A, E | A, F | A, G | B, C |
| C, D | C, F | C, G | D, E | D, G | F, G | |

Find out how the seven people can sit round the table so that each person knows the two people on either side of them.

# Money matters : income tax

The government spends a lot of money each year, on such things as education, health, defence, and so on. Much of this money comes from **income tax**. The amount which anyone has to pay depends on their income – the amount of money they have coming in.

People do not pay tax on the whole of their income. There is part of their income which they are allowed to keep without any tax being deducted from it. This part is called their **allowances**. The size of the allowances depends on a whole variety of things.

## Find out

It is possible for someone to have an income and not pay any income tax.

Find out what is the most you can earn without having to pay tax.

The **rate** at which you pay tax depends on how much you earn.
Your taxable income (your income minus allowances) is 'sliced' into **tax bands**. Each band is taxed at a different rate.

This diagram shows the tax bands and tax rates in 1986–87.

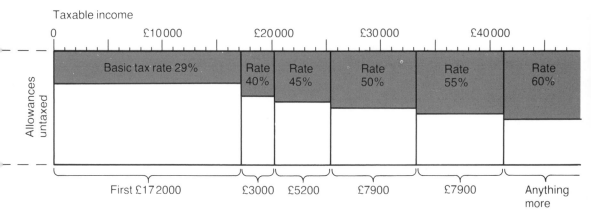

**Find out**

Find out what the tax bands are at the moment.

Work out how much tax is paid altogether by someone with a taxable income of £50000.

**Tax facts**

- The 'tax year' (the year for which your income is calculated for tax purposes) runs from 6th April in one year to 5th April in the next year.

  Before 1752, rents and taxes of all kinds were calculated up to the end of the first quarter of the year – 25th March, called 'Lady Day'.

  In 1752 an adjustment was made to the calendar, so that 2nd September was followed by 14th September. So from Lady Day 1752 to Lady Day 1753 there were only 354 days.
  The Treasury accounting system could not cope with that, so from 1753 taxes were collected 11 days later, on 5th April!

  When income tax was first introduced in 1799, 5th April was the date on which it was collected.

- For nearly 30 years in the 19th century there was no income tax.
  It started again in 1842. The rate was 3%!

- In 1875 the rate of income tax was down to 0·83%.

- The highest the (basic) rate has ever been was during the Second World War, when it was 50%.

- There are two small islands around the British Isles where no income tax is paid by the inhabitants – Lundy Island and Sark.

# 3 Fractions

## A Halves, quarters, eighths, . . .

Some British firms still use inches for measuring lengths.

This line is 1 inch long: ⊢————————⊣

The symbol for inches is ″. So 3″ means 3 inches.

To measure lengths which are shorter than 1″, an inch can be
divided in half, then in half again, and again, and so on.

Here is half of an inch.   $\frac{1}{2}$″

Half of $\frac{1}{2}$″ is $\frac{1}{4}$″.   $\frac{1}{4}$″

Half of $\frac{1}{4}$″ is $\frac{1}{8}$″.   $\frac{1}{8}$″

Half of $\frac{1}{8}$″ is $\frac{1}{16}$″.   $\frac{1}{16}$″

This enlarged diagram of an inch shows all the halves, quarters, and so on.

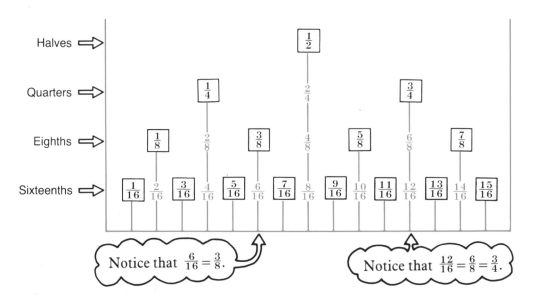

Notice that $\frac{6}{16} = \frac{3}{8}$.

Notice that $\frac{12}{16} = \frac{6}{8} = \frac{3}{4}$.

18

The fractions shown in **black** on the diagram are the ones used to name the parts of an inch.

So for example instead of $\frac{10}{16}''$, we would write $\frac{5}{8}''$.

Instead of $\frac{4}{8}''$, we would write $\frac{1}{2}''$.

A1 Write down the length of each line shown below, as a fraction of an inch. (Try to do them without looking at the diagram on the opposite page.)

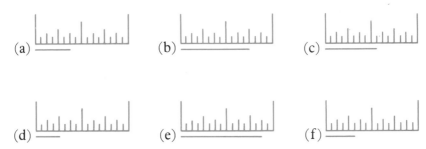

If you do not have a diagram like the one on the opposite page, you can still change sixteenths to eighths, and so on.

You divide the top and bottom of the fraction by 2, like this:

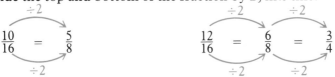

When you cannot go any further, the fraction is then in its **simplest form** (or its **lowest terms**).

A2 Re-write each of these fractions in its simplest form.
Do them without looking at the diagram on the opposite page.
(a) $\frac{4}{8}$    (b) $\frac{4}{16}$    (c) $\frac{6}{16}$    (d) $\frac{12}{16}$    (e) $\frac{2}{8}$

It is often useful to be able to go the other way, and change halves, quarters and eighths into sixteenths.

To do this you multiply the top and bottom by 2, until you get sixteenths.

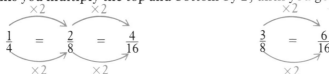

A3 Change each of these fractions into sixteenths.
(a) $\frac{3}{4}$    (b) $\frac{5}{8}$    (c) $\frac{1}{2}$    (d) $\frac{7}{8}$

**A4** Sally wants to tighten a nut on her bike.

A $\frac{1}{4}''$ spanner is too small.

A $\frac{3}{8}''$ spanner is too big.

Sally needs a spanner between $\frac{1}{4}''$ and $\frac{3}{8}''$.

(a) Change $\frac{1}{4}''$ to sixteenths.

(b) Change $\frac{3}{8}''$ to sixteenths.

(c) Write down the size of a spanner which is halfway between $\frac{1}{4}''$ and $\frac{3}{8}''$.

**A5** Which of the rods shown below are too big to go through a hole whose diameter is $\frac{5}{8}''$?

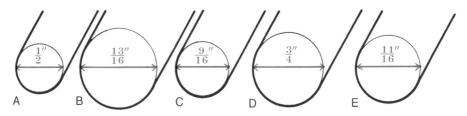

## Adding halves, quarters, eighths and sixteenths

You can easily add halves, quarters, eighths and sixteenths by changing them all to sixteenths (or sometimes eighths).

**Worked example**

Work out $\frac{3}{8} + \frac{5}{16}$.

Change $\frac{3}{8}$ to sixteenths: $\frac{3}{8} = \frac{6}{16}$.

So $\frac{3}{8} + \frac{5}{16} = \frac{6}{16} + \frac{5}{16} = \frac{11}{16}$.

**A6** Work these out.

(a) $\frac{1}{4} + \frac{1}{16}$     (b) $\frac{1}{2} + \frac{5}{16}$     (c) $\frac{5}{8} + \frac{3}{16}$     (d) $\frac{1}{4} + \frac{3}{8}$

(e) $\frac{7}{8} - \frac{1}{16}$ (Subtract!)     (f) $\frac{5}{8} - \frac{3}{16}$     (g) $\frac{1}{2} - \frac{3}{8}$

## B Equal fractions

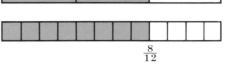

$\frac{2}{3}$ of this strip has been coloured. ➡

This strip has been split into 12 equal parts. ➡
8 parts are coloured.
So $\frac{8}{12}$ of the strip is coloured.

You can see that the same amount of the strip has been coloured
in each diagram. So $\frac{2}{3} = \frac{8}{12}$.

We can get from $\frac{2}{3}$ to $\frac{8}{12}$ by multiplying the top and bottom numbers by 4.

$$\overset{\times 4}{\underset{\times 4}{\frac{2}{3} = \frac{8}{12}}}$$

If we start with any fractions, and multiply the top and bottom by the
**same number**, we get a fraction which is equal to the first one.

For example,

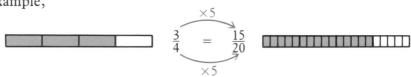

$$\overset{\times 5}{\underset{\times 5}{\frac{3}{4} = \frac{15}{20}}}$$

**B1** Copy and complete these.

(a) $\frac{2}{5} = \frac{}{20}$    (b) $\frac{3}{8} = \frac{}{32}$    (c) $\frac{5}{6} = \frac{}{18}$    (d) $\frac{1}{3} = \frac{}{27}$

(e) $\frac{4}{5} = \frac{16}{}$    (f) $\frac{2}{3} = \frac{10}{}$    (g) $\frac{3}{7} = \frac{}{21}$    (h) $\frac{4}{5} = \frac{}{100}$

We can reverse the process. If we divide the top and bottom of a fraction
by the same number, we get an equal fraction.

For example,

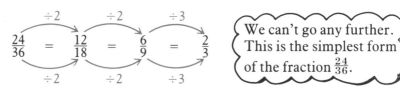

$$\overset{\div 2 \quad \div 2 \quad \div 3}{\underset{\div 2 \quad \div 2 \quad \div 3}{\frac{24}{36} = \frac{12}{18} = \frac{6}{9} = \frac{2}{3}}}$$

We can't go any further.
This is the simplest form
of the fraction $\frac{24}{36}$.

**B2** Write each of these fractions in its simplest form.

(a) $\frac{12}{15}$   (b) $\frac{10}{40}$   (c) $\frac{25}{30}$   (d) $\frac{16}{24}$   (e) $\frac{15}{25}$   (f) $\frac{40}{100}$

## C  Dividing an amount in a given ratio

Here is an extract from Grandma's will.

> I leave £600 to my grandchildren Ruth and David, to be divided between them in the ratio of their ages when I die.

If Grandma dies now, Ruth is 3 years old and David 2 years old.
So the £600 has to be divided between them in the **ratio 3 to 2**.
In other words, for every £3 Ruth gets, David gets £2.

You can see from the diagram that Ruth's share will be $\frac{3}{5}$ of the money and David's share will be $\frac{2}{5}$.

(Out of every £5, Ruth gets £3 and David £2).

Ruth's share     David's share

So Ruth will get $\frac{3}{5}$ of £600 = **£360**, and David will get $\frac{2}{5}$ of £600 = **£240**.

**C1**  Suppose Grandma dies 5 years later, when Ruth is 8 and David is 7.

Calculate the amounts which Ruth and David will get.

**C2**  Suppose Grandma dies when Ruth is 13 and David 12.
Calculate the amounts which each will get.

**C3**  Jim makes pink paint by mixing red and white in the ratio 5 to 4 (5 litres of red to 4 litres of white).

Jim has made 72 litres of pink paint. How much red and how much white did he use?

**C4**  Amin and Ron go into business together. Amin invests £25 000 in the business and Ron invests £15 000.
They agree to share the profits in the ratio of their investments.

(a) What fraction of the profits will Amin get, and what fraction will Ron get?

(b) In the first year, the business makes a profit of £6000. How much does each partner get?

**C5**  Karen and Judith set up a health food shop. Karen puts £8000 into the business and Judith £12 000. They agree to share the profits in the ratio of their investments.

(a) What fraction of the profits will each partner get?

(b) If the profits amount to £7500, how much will each get?

C6  PVA glue is very popular for gluing wood and other materials.
It can also be mixed with water for other purposes. The information
below comes from the label of a tin of PVA glue.

| Purpose | PVA | Water |
|---------|-----|-------|
| Sealing dusty ceilings and floors | 1 | 5 |
| Priming gloss paint before wallpapering | 1 | 1 |
| Sealing end-grain wood | 5 | 1 |
| Stiffening fabrics | 1 | 19 |

(a)  How much water should be mixed with 250 ml of PVA when
stiffening fabric?

(b)  A floor needs 30 litres of mixture to seal it. How much PVA
and how much water are needed?

(c)  15 litres of mixture are needed to prime some gloss paint before
wallpapering. How much PVA and how much water should be used?

(d)  A carpenter decides to make up 3 litres of mixture for sealing
end-grain wood. How much PVA and water are required?

C7  Kate, Cheryl and Pauline cleared a garden of rubbish, weeded it
and dug it over. Here is a record of who worked when.

|         | Mon | Tues | Wed | Thurs | Fri |
|---------|-----|------|-----|-------|-----|
| Kate    | ✓   | ✓    |     | ✓     |     |
| Cheryl  | ✓   |      | ✓   | ✓     | ✓   |
| Pauline |     | ✓    | ✓   |       | ✓   |

Altogether they earned £450. Suggest how they should share
it out, and work out their shares.

C8  Manoj, David and Ronnie re-wired a house and agreed to share
the amount they earned in the ratio 3 to 4 to 5.
They earned £300 altogether. Calculate their shares.

**Concrete**

Concrete is made from cement powder, sand and gravel.
The cement, sand and gravel are mixed with water, but
the water dries out later and the concrete 'sets'.

Each type of concrete can be described by giving the
ratios, or **proportions**, of cement, sand and gravel.
One commonly used concrete is called '1 to 3 to 6' concrete.
The proportions here are by **volume**: 1 bucketful of cement
is mixed with 3 bucketfuls of sand and 6 bucketfuls of gravel.

When the concrete is mixed, the total volume decreases by
about one-third.

23

# 4 Trigonometry (2)

## A  Tangent: a review

In chapter 1 we used the formula

side adjacent to θ × tan θ = side opposite θ

to calculate the side opposite angle θ in a right-angled triangle.

We can use the abbreviations 'adj' and 'opp', and write the formula

adj × tan θ = opp

The questions below are for practice in using this formula.

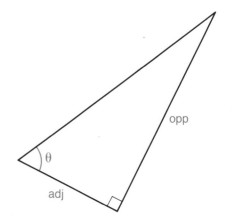

**A1**  Calculate the sides marked with letters in these right-angled triangles.

(a)

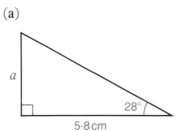

(b)

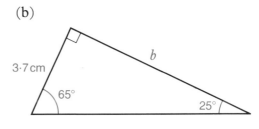

**A2**  Calculate

(a)  the length marked *a*

(b)  the height marked *h*

in the diagram on the right.

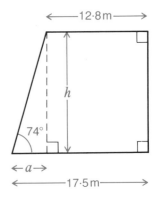

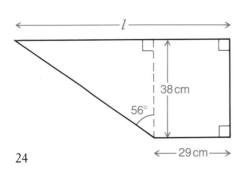

**A3**  Calculate the length marked *l* in the diagram on the left.

## B Calculating the side adjacent to an angle

So far we have used the formula adj × tan θ = opp to calculate the side opposite angle θ.

We can also use the formula to calculate 'adj' when we know 'opp'.

**Worked example**

Calculate the side marked $x$ in this right-angled triangle.

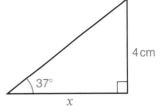

4 cm

37°

$x$

From the formula 'adj × tan θ = opp' we know that $x \times \tan 37° = 4$.

Divide both sides by tan 37°: $\dfrac{x \times \tan 37°}{\tan 37°} = \dfrac{4}{\tan 37°}$

So $x = \dfrac{4}{\tan 37°}$

On most calculators you can do 4 ÷ tan 37° like this:

Enter 4 → Press ÷ → Enter 37 → Press tan → Press =

The result should be 5·3 cm to 1 d.p.

(You can see from the rough sketch above that $x$ must be greater than 4 cm. You can use this as a check on the result.)

**B1** In each case below, use the formula
adj × tan θ = opp
to write down an equation with the unknown side in it.
Then solve the equation, correct to 1 d.p.
(The first one is started for you.)

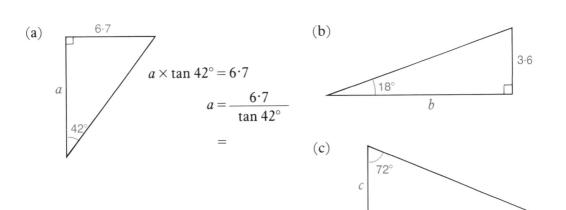

(a)

6·7

$a$

42°

$a \times \tan 42° = 6·7$

$a = \dfrac{6·7}{\tan 42°}$

$=$

(b)

3·6

18°

$b$

(c)

72°

$c$

10·5

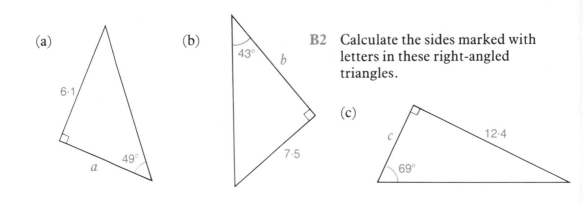

(a)

6·1

49°

a

(b)

43°

b

7·5

**B2** Calculate the sides marked with letters in these right-angled triangles.

(c)

12·4

c

69°

**B3** Calculate the sides marked with letters in these triangles.
Be careful: sometimes the lettered side is opposite the given angle, and sometimes it is adjacent to it.

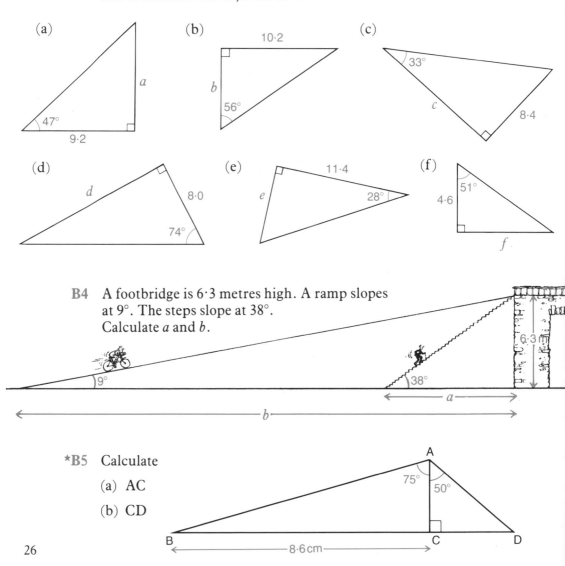

(a)

a

47°

9·2

(b)

10·2

b

56°

(c)

33°

c

8·4

(d)

d

8·0

74°

(e)

11·4

e

28°

(f)

51°

4·6

f

**B4** A footbridge is 6·3 metres high. A ramp slopes at 9°. The steps slope at 38°.
Calculate a and b.

9°

38°

6·3 m

a

b

*B5 Calculate

(a) AC

(b) CD

A

75°

50°

B

8·6 cm

C

D

## C  Inverse tangents

So far we have used tangents to solve two kinds of problem connected with right-angled triangles:
(1)  calculating the side opposite an angle, when the angle and the side adjacent to it are known;
(2)  calculating the side adjacent to an angle, when the angle and the side opposite it are known.

There is a third kind of problem as well:
(3)  calculating an angle when the sides opposite it and adjacent to it are known.

Here is an example of this kind of problem.
$\theta$ is unknown.
The side adjacent to $\theta$ is 4 cm.
The side opposite $\theta$ is 2 cm.

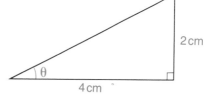

We know that $\qquad\qquad$ adj $\times \tan \theta = $ opp

so it follows that $\qquad\qquad$ $4 \times \tan \theta = 2$

Divide both sides by 4. $\qquad$ $\dfrac{4 \times \tan \theta}{4} = \dfrac{2}{4}$

$$\tan \theta = 0{\cdot}5$$

Now we have to find the angle whose tangent is $0{\cdot}5$.

On a calculator we know how to start with an angle and find its tangent. Now we need to carry out the **inverse** process: starting with the tangent and finding the angle.

On many calculators there is a key marked $\boxed{\text{inv}}$ for this.

If you know the tangent is $0{\cdot}5$, you find the angle like this:

Result **26·565 . . .**
(On some calculators instead of $\boxed{\text{inv}}$ you press $\boxed{\text{arc}}$ or $\boxed{\text{2nd F}}$ .
Find out how yours works.)

The angle whose tangent is $0{\cdot}5$ is $26{\cdot}6°$ (to 1 d.p.).
We can write this in two ways.

$\qquad$ $\tan 26{\cdot}6° = 0{\cdot}5$ $\qquad$ inv $\tan 0{\cdot}5 = 26{\cdot}6°$

$\qquad$ C1 $\quad$ Use a calculator to find (to 1 d.p.) the angle whose tangent is $0{\cdot}6$.

$\qquad$ C2 $\quad$ What angles have these tangents?
$\qquad\qquad$ (a) $0{\cdot}75$ $\quad$ (b) $1{\cdot}35$ $\quad$ (c) $0{\cdot}08$ $\quad$ (d) $37{\cdot}1$ $\quad$ (e) $213$

27

**C3** Enter 43 into your calculator, press [tan] and then [inv][tan] .
You should get back to 43. Try it with other angles.

## Worked example

Calculate the angle marked $x$ in this triangle.

First label the sides 'hyp', 'opp' and 'adj'.

Write down the basic formula:

$$adj \times \tan x = opp.$$

We get $\quad 7 \times \tan x = 4,$

$$\tan x = \frac{4}{7}.$$

On the calculator, we do $4 \div 7$ and press [=].
We get $0 \cdot 571428 \ldots$ This is the value of **tan $x$**.

$$\tan x = 0 \cdot 571428 \ldots$$

To find $x$ we need the **inverse tangent** of $0 \cdot 571428 \ldots$, or in other words the angle whose tangent is $0 \cdot 571428 \ldots$

So we leave the number $0 \cdot 571428 \ldots$ in the calculator and press [inv] [tan].
We get $29 \cdot 7448 \ldots$

So $x = \mathbf{29 \cdot 7°}$ to 1 d.p.

**C4** Calculate the angles marked with letters in these triangles, to the nearest $0 \cdot 1°$.

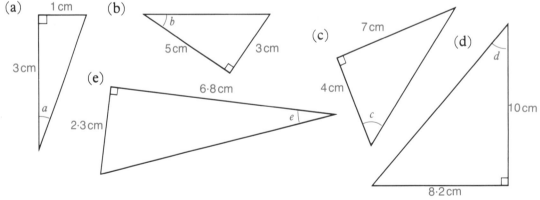

(a) 1 cm  (b)  (c) 7 cm  (d)

3 cm  (e)  6·8 cm  4 cm  10 cm

$a$  2·3 cm  5 cm  3 cm  $b$  $e$  $c$  8·2 cm  $d$

**C5** This is the end wall of a house.
It is symmetrical about the dotted line.

Calculate, to the nearest degree, the angle $\theta$ at which the roof slopes.

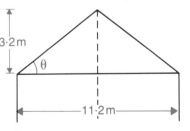

3·2 m  $\theta$  11·2 m

28

**C6** A windmill W is 5·3 km north of a farmhouse F, and 6·6 km east of F.

Calculate, to the nearest degree, the bearing of W from F (the angle marked $b$ in the diagram).

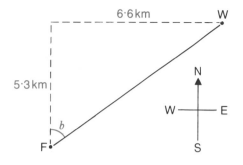

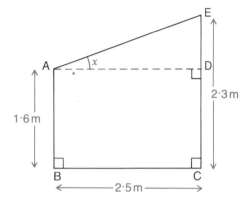

**C7** The drawing on the right shows the end wall of a shed.

    (a) Calculate DE.

    (b) Calculate the angle which the roof makes with the horizontal (the angle marked $x$). Give the angle to the nearest degree.

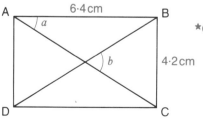

**C8** The shape on the left is symmetrical about the dotted line.

    (a) Calculate RS.

    (b) Calculate the angle marked $\theta$, to the nearest 0·1°.

**C9** Triangle ABC is isosceles: AB = AC.

    (a) Calculate the angle marked $x$, to the nearest 0·1°.

    (b) Calculate angle BAC.

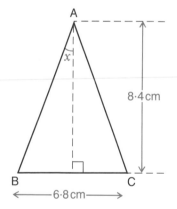

**★C10** ABCD is a rectangle. Calculate
    (a) the angle $a$ between AB and AC
    (b) the angle $b$ between AC and DB

29

## D Miscellaneous questions

**D1** Calculate the sides and angles marked with letters in these right-angled triangles.

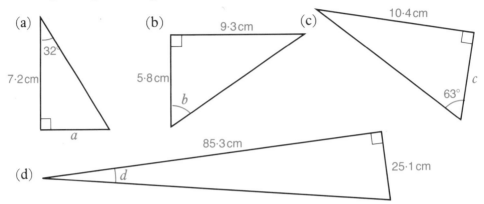

(a)   (b)   (c)

(d)

**D2** This diagram shows the cross-section of a motorway cutting.

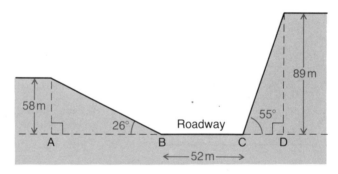

(a) Calculate AB, to the nearest metre.

(b) Calculate CD, to the nearest metre.

(c) What is the total width of the cutting (the length AD)?

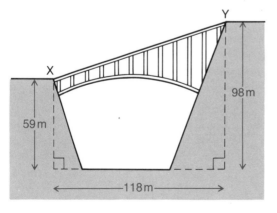

**D3** This is another motorway cutting, with a footbridge linking the two sides.

Calculate the angle at which the line XY slopes to the horizontal.

(Hint: Imagine a horizontal line through X which meets the vertical line through Y.)

# 5 Direct proportionality

## A  The unitary method

If you have some emulsion paint for painting walls, the area you can paint is **proportional** to the amount of paint you have.

With twice as much paint you can paint twice the area. With three times as much paint you can paint three times the area, and so on.

A1  Pavel is painting the inside walls of a scout hut. So far he has used up 5 litres of paint and he has covered an area of $24\,m^2$.

(a)  What area will 10 litres of paint cover?

(b)  What area will 30 litres of paint cover?

(c)  How much paint will cover $240\,m^2$?

The **unitary method** can be used in calculations involving quantities which are proportional to one another.
Here is an example.

**Worked example**.

The cost of running an electric heater is proportional to the time for which the heater is on.
If it costs 45p to run the heater for 6·5 hours, how much will it cost to run it for 10 hours?

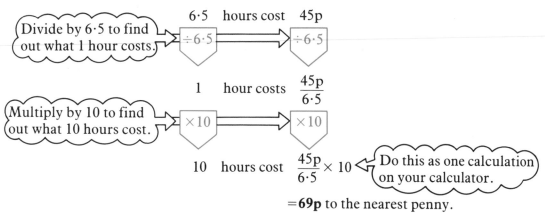

6·5  hours cost  45p

Divide by 6·5 to find out what 1 hour costs.  ÷6·5  ÷6·5

1  hour costs  $\dfrac{45p}{6\cdot5}$

Multiply by 10 to find out what 10 hours cost.  ×10  ×10

10  hours cost  $\dfrac{45p}{6\cdot5} \times 10$  Do this as one calculation on your calculator.

=**69p** to the nearest penny.

A2  The weight of concrete is proportional to its volume. If $3\cdot5\,m^3$ of concrete weighs 8·4 tonnes, what does $4\cdot5\,m^3$ weigh?

**A3** When a metal girder is heated, it expands (gets longer). For a particular girder, the amount by which it expands is proportional to the rise in temperature.

If a 16 degree temperature rise causes a girder to expand by 0·36 cm, what expansion is caused by a 24 degree rise?

**A4** The energy content (in calories) of a food is proportional to the weight of it eaten.

(a) 50 g of butter provides 370 calories. How many calories does 80 g provide?

(b) 25 g of white bread provides 63 calories. How many calories does 400 g provide?

**A5** It took Karen 2 hours and 20 minutes to type a 15-page document. How long will it take her to type a 24-page document of a similar kind?

**A6** It takes 7 hours 40 minutes to walk 15 miles over moorland. If you walked for $4\frac{1}{2}$ hours in similar conditions, how far would you go?

## B  The multiplier method

This is another method of doing calculations like those in the previous questions.
Here we show how the worked example on the previous page can also be done by the multiplier method.

**Worked example**

It costs 45p to run a heater for 6·5 hours. How much will it cost for 10 hours?

Here is the information in a table.

| 6·5 hours | 10 hours |
|-----------|----------|
| 45p | ? |

We know the cost for 6·5 hours. We want the cost for 10 hours.
What has the time been multiplied by, as we go from 6·5 to 10?

To find out, we divide 10 by 6·5.   $\dfrac{10}{6·5}$ = **1·538** . . .

$\times\ 1·538$ . . .

| 6·5 hours | 10 hours |
|-----------|----------|
| 45p | ? |

$\times\ 1·538$ . . .

Now we have to multiply the cost also by 1·538 . . .
So the cost for 10 hours is  45p × 1·538 . . . = **69p**, to the nearest penny.

32

Use the multiplier method to do questions B1 to B7.

**B1**   25 g of Marmite contains 2 g of salt.
What weight of Marmite contains 100 g of salt?

**B2**   25 g of cornflakes provide 90 calories. What weight of cornflakes will provide 500 calories?

**B3**   100 g of milk contains 0·05 g of salt.
A normal person in a temperate climate needs 4 g of salt per day. How much milk would you need to drink in a day to get all your intake of salt from milk alone?

The multipliers in a proportionality calculation may be less than 1.

**Worked example**

50 g of cheese contains 405 mg (milligrams) of calcium.
What weight of cheese contains 100 mg of calcium?

Here is the information in a table.

| Cheese | 50 g | ? |
|---|---|---|
| Calcium | 405 mg | 100 mg |

The multiplier from 405 mg to 100 mg            × 0·246. . .

is $\dfrac{100}{405} = 0·246$ . . .

So we multiply the 50 g by 0·246 . . .
The weight of cheese is  0·246 . . . × 50 g = **12·3 g** (to 3 s.f.)

**B4**   25 g of white flour contains 36 mg of calcium.
What weight of flour contains 20 mg of calcium?

**B5**   A rise in temperature of 11·5 degrees caused a girder to expand by 0·36 cm.

What rise in temperature will cause an expansion of 0·25 cm?

**B6**   100 g of bacon provides 475 calories.
How much bacon do you need to take in 200 calories?

**B7**   100 g of Cheddar cheese contains 25·5 g of protein. How much cheese will contain 10 g of protein?

The ordinary kind of proportionality, where multiplying one quantity means multiplying the other by the same number, is called **direct** proportionality.

This is to distinguish it from another kind, which we shall look at in chapter 7.

## C Enlargement: scaling up

The editor of a magazine wants to print an enlargement of this photo in the magazine.

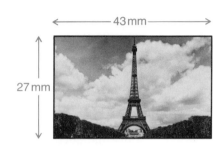

To fit the page, the enlarged photo has to be 110 mm wide.

The editor needs to calculate the height of the enlarged photo (because she needs to know how much space there will be below it).

The multiplier method can be used to calculate the new height.

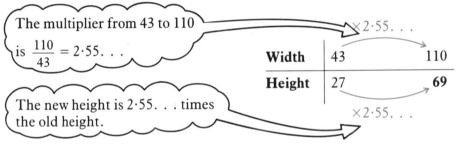

The multiplier from 43 to 110 is $\frac{110}{43} = 2.55\ldots$

The new height is $2.55\ldots$ times the old height.

|            |    | $\times 2.55\ldots$ |
|------------|----|----|
| **Width**  | 43 | 110 |
| **Height** | 27 | 69 |

$\times 2.55\ldots$

Notice that the multiplier is the **scale factor** of the enlargement.

It is calculated by doing $\dfrac{\text{new width}}{\text{old width}}$.

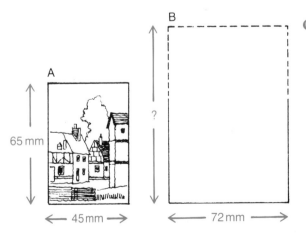

**C1** Picture A is to be enlarged to fit the frame B. The problem is to work out the height of B.

(a) Use the widths of A and B to calculate the scale factor of the enlargement.

(b) Multiply the height of A by the scale factor to find the height of B.

**C2** Picture C is to be enlarged to fit the frame D.

Calculate

(a) the scale factor of the enlargement

(b) the width of D

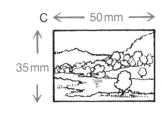

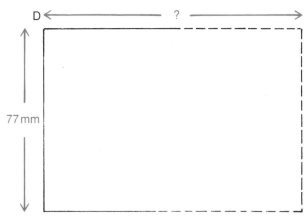

**C3** A photo is 80 mm wide and 105 mm high.
It is to be enlarged so that the enlargement is 280 mm wide.

(a) Calculate the scale factor of the enlargement.

(b) Calculate the height of the enlarged photo.

**C4** A rare foreign stamp is 3·2 cm by 2·4 cm.
An artist wants to put an enlargement of the stamp on to a poster to advertise an exhibition.

If the longer side of the enlargement is 28 cm, what is the length of the shorter side?

**C5** Can this photo be enlarged to fit the frame? Explain how you get your answer.

# D Reduction: scaling down

When the scale factor is **less than 1**, we get a **reduction**.
Picture B is a reduction of picture A. The scale factor is 0·6.

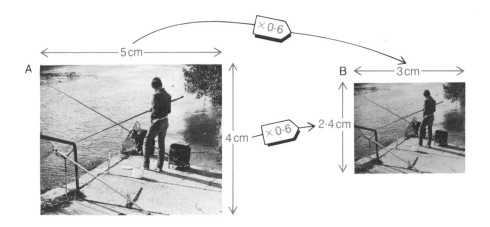

If you did not know the scale factor, you could work it out from the measurements.

For example, 5 cm is reduced to 3 cm.

So the scale factor $= \dfrac{\text{New measurement}}{\text{Old measurement}} = \dfrac{3}{5} = 0\cdot6.$

**D1** Calculate the scale factor of this reduction

    (a) by measuring the longer sides     (b) by measuring the shorter sides

    (c) by measuring across from corner to corner

**D2** A picture measures 88 cm by 65 cm.

Can the picture be reduced to fit a frame which is 57 cm by 40 cm?
Explain how you get your answer.

**D3** Picture A is to be reduced to fit the frame B.

A

5·3 cm

←————6·2 cm————→

B

3·4 cm

←————?————→

(a) Use the shorter sides of the picture and the frame to calculate the scale factor of the reduction.

(b) Calculate the longer side of the reduced frame.

**D4** A picture 25·2 cm wide and 16·4 cm high is to be reduced to fit a frame which is 14·8 cm wide.

Calculate the height of the frame.

**D5** A poster measuring 96·5 cm by 55·2 cm is to be reduced to make a picture postcard. The longer dimension of the postcard is 17·5 cm. What is the shorter dimension?

**D6** The model village in Bourton-on-the-Water in Gloucestershire is a model of Bourton itself.

The scale factor of the reduction is $\frac{1}{9}$.

(a) Estimate the height of the tower of the model church.

(b) Use your estimate to estimate the height of the tower of the real church.

**D7** The model village in Bourton is a model of Bourton itself. So in the model village there is a model of the model village!

Estimate the height of the tower of the church in the model of the model village.

# Money matters: VAT

The things which people spend their money on can be divided up
into **goods** and **services**.

| | |
|---|---|
| 'Goods' are the things you buy from shops or mail order firms, such as food, clothes, records, computers, and so on. | 'Services' are things that other people do for you, such as repair your bike or TV set. |

VAT is a tax which is charged on most goods and services.
The tax goes to the government to help pay the cost of running the
country.

For some goods you do not have to pay VAT.
Examples are books and take away cold foods.

| DUMPLINGS | PRICE LIST | |
|---|---|---|
| | Eat here | Take out |
| Plain . . . . . | 80p | 70p |
| Beef . . . . | £1·03 | 90p |
| Apple . . . . | 86p | 75p |
| Banana . . . | 92p | 80p |

The rate of VAT is fixed by the government. The rate may be
changed from time to time. If there is a change, it is usually
announced in an annual Budget in March.

Suppose the rate of VAT is 15%. You want to buy a bike whose
price excluding VAT is £80.
If you buy the bike you will be charged £80 + 15% of £80 = £80 + £12 = **£92**.

1 Find out the present rate of VAT. Work out the cost,
including VAT, of an item whose price excluding VAT is

(a) £10   (b) £20   (c) £50   (d) £55   (e) £58·50

Suppose you are in business. You buy materials, from which you make things to sell to other people.

You pay VAT when you buy the materials, but **you get this back from the taxman**.

What happens is illustrated in this story.

**The story:** Alan sells Brenda the wood to make a dog kennel.
Brenda makes the kennel, and sells it to Colin, who paints it.
Diana buys the kennel from Colin.

The rate of VAT at the time is 10%.

Brenda buys the wood from Alan.
Alan charges £20 + VAT = **£22**.

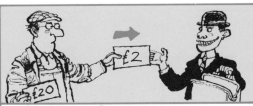

Alan keeps £20.
He pays £2 VAT to the taxman.

Colin buys the kennel from Brenda.
Brenda charges £60 + VAT = **£66**.

Brenda keeps £60.
She pays the £6 VAT to the taxman.
She gets back the £2 VAT she paid on the wood.

Diana buys the kennel from Colin.
Colin charges £100 + VAT = **£110**

Colin keeps £100.
He pays the £10 VAT to the taxman.
He gets back the £6 VAT he paid on the kennel.

At each stage the taxman collects 10% of the **value added** to the kennel.
For example, Colin buys it for £60 and sells it for £100.
The value added is £40, so the taxman gets £4 from Colin. (Colin gives him £10 but gets £6 back.)

At the end of the story, the taxman has made a gain of £10, which is 10% of the final selling price of the kennel.

# Review 1

## 1 Trigonometry (1)

**1.1** Calculate the sides marked with letters in these right-angled triangles, to the nearest 0·1 cm.

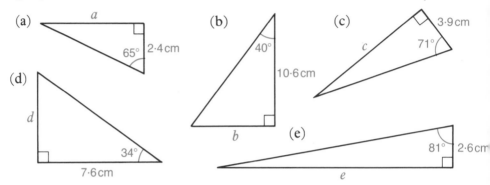

(a)  *a*  65°  2·4 cm

(b)  40°  10·6 cm  *b*

(c)  *c*  71°  3·9 cm

(d)  *d*  34°  7·6 cm

(e)  *e*  81°  2·6 cm

**1.2** Calculate the height marked *h*, to the nearest 0·1 m.

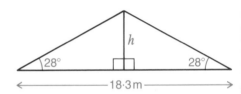

28°  *h*  28°  18·3 m

## 2 Arranging and selecting (1)

**2.1** Mary, Jeff, Hitesh, Karen, Gary and Sadia are six pupils in a school. The following pairs are friends:

Mary and Sadia, Jeff and Hitesh, Jeff and Karen, Jeff and Gary, Karen and Hitesh, Karen and Sadia.

(a) Can they sit down in a row of six seats so that people sitting next to one another are friends? How many different ways are there to seat them?

(b) Can they sit in a circle so that each person has a friend on either side?

Jeff falls out with Hitesh, so they don't want to sit next to each other. Mary and Gary fall in love.

(c) Is it now possible for the six people to sit in a row? In how many ways can they be seated?

(d) Is it now possible for them to sit in a circle?

(e) Could they sit in a circle if Hitesh and Sadia became friends? In how many ways can they be seated?

2.2 Four clerks work in an office. Each one is entitled to 3 weeks' holiday, but not more than 2 weeks can be taken in any one stretch. They all have to take their holidays within a period of 6 weeks, but not more than two of the clerks are allowed to be away at the same time.

(a) Make a holiday timetable for them.
(b) Explain why it would be impossible to squeeze all their holidays into a 5-week period.

# 3 Fractions

3.1 Change to sixteenths (a) $\frac{3}{8}$ (b) $\frac{3}{4}$ (c) $\frac{1}{2}$ (d) $\frac{7}{8}$

3.2 Calculate (a) $\frac{1}{8} + \frac{1}{2}$ (b) $\frac{3}{16} + \frac{5}{8}$ (c) $\frac{3}{4} - \frac{5}{16}$ (d) $\frac{9}{16} - \frac{3}{8}$

3.3 Which fraction is halfway between

(a) $\frac{5}{8}$ and $\frac{3}{4}$ (b) $\frac{3}{4}$ and 1 (c) $\frac{3}{8}$ and $\frac{1}{2}$ (d) $\frac{1}{8}$ and $\frac{1}{4}$

3.4 Divide £48 between two people in the ratio

(a) 5 to 3 (b) 7 to 3 (c) 5 to 1

# 4 Trigonometry (2)

4.1 Calculate the sides marked with letters in these right-angled triangles, to the nearest 0·1 cm.

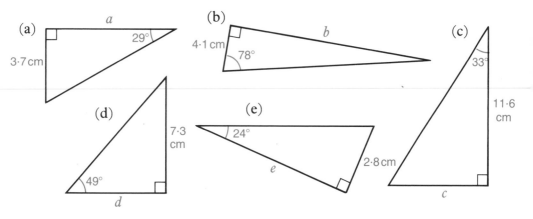

4.2 Calculate the angles marked with letters, to the nearest degree.

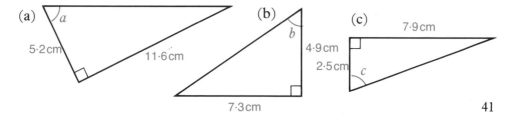

4.3 (a) Calculate the height of an equilateral triangle whose sides are each 5 cm long, correct to the nearest 0·1 cm.

(b) Calculate the area of the triangle, to the nearest 0·1 cm².

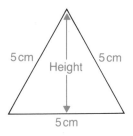

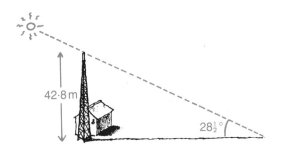

4.4 If the sun's angle of elevation is $28\frac{1}{2}°$, calculate

(a) the length of the shadow of a mast 42·8 m tall

(b) the height of a tower whose shadow is 164·5 m long

# 5 Direct proportionality

5.1 If the gas in a closed container is heated, its pressure increases. (Pressure can be measured in millibars, mb.) The increase in the pressure is proportional to the rise in temperature.

If a temperature rise of 80 degrees causes the pressure to increase by 650 mb, what increase in pressure will occur when the temperature rises by 150 degrees?

5.2 The distance by rail from London Euston to Crewe is 158 miles. The ordinary single fare (in 1987) was £22·50. The distance from Euston to Carlisle is 299 miles. If fares are proportional to distances, what would the fare to Carlisle be? (In actual fact the fare was £37·00).

5.3 Picture E is to be enlarged to fit the frame F. Calculate the height of F, showing how you do it.

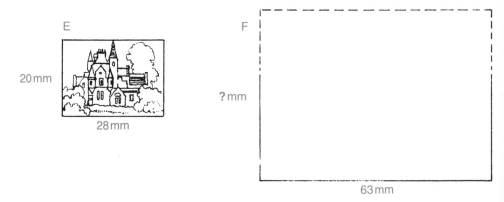

# 6 Arranging and selecting (2)

## A Combining choices

**A1** This is the lunch menu at a roadside café.

Customers choose one of the three first courses and one of the two second courses.

What different two-course meals can be chosen from the menu?

(Use F to stand for Fish and chips, etc.)

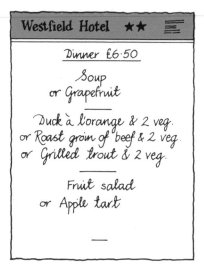

**Alf's Café**

Lunch £1·50

Fish and Chips
or Ham Salad
or Steak pie + chips

Rice pudding
or
Ice cream

**A2** This is the lunch menu at a high-class hotel.

What different two-course meals can be chosen from this menu?

**Westfield Hotel ★★**

Lunch £3·50

Grilled plaice, chipped potatoes
or York ham with salad
or Home cooked steak pie
or Spaghetti bolognaise

Fruit Salad
or Chocolate gateau
or Sherry trifle

**A3** This is the dinner menu from the same hotel.

Customers choose a first course, a second course and a third course.

How many different three-course meals can be chosen?

**Westfield Hotel ★★**

Dinner £6·50

Soup
or Grapefruit

Duck à l'orange & 2 veg.
or Roast groin of beef & 2 veg.
or Grilled trout & 2 veg.

Fruit salad
or Apple tart

## B  Listing possibilities

Here is another lunch menu.

Suppose we want to make a list of all the different meals it is possible to have.

We could try just writing them down in any old order, until we couldn't think of any more.
But it is better to have a **method** for making a list, so that we can be **sure** that none have been left out.

One good method is to use a **branching diagram** (also called a **tree diagram**).

This is how it works.

*Lamb chop e 2 veg.*
*or Shepherd's pie . e 2 veg.*
*or Hamburgers e 2 veg.*

*Apricot pie e Custard*
*or Jelly e Cream*
*or Banana Split*

**1** We show the three choices of main course like this.
(L stands for 'lamb chop', etc.)

L

S

H

**2** L (lamb) can be followed by A (apricot), J (jelly) or B (banana). We show them like this.

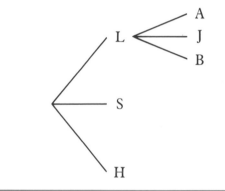

**3** S can be followed by A, J or B. H can be followed by A, J or B. We show them like this.

**4** Now we can list all the possible meals by following the lines across the diagram.

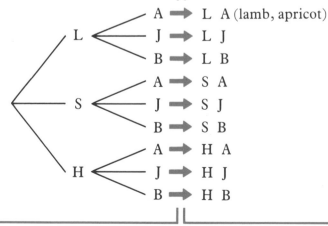

L  A ➡ L A (lamb, apricot)
J ➡ L J
B ➡ L B
A ➡ S A
J ➡ S J
B ➡ S B
A ➡ H A
J ➡ H J
B ➡ H B

9 possible meals altogether

**B1** (a) Make a branching diagram to show all the possible meals which can be chosen from this menu.

Start like this:

Fish and chips
or Sausage and chips
or Cheese salad
or Ham salad

Treade pudding
or Apple pie

(b) Use your diagram to make a list of all the different possible meals. The list begins F T   F A . . .

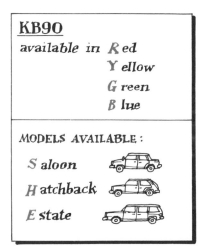

**KB90**

available in  R ed
                    Y ellow
                    G reen
                    B lue

MODELS AVAILABLE :

S aloon
H atchback
E state

**B2** People who want to buy the new KB90 car have a choice of four colours: red, yellow, green or blue.

They also have a choice of three models: saloon, hatchback or estate.

(a) Copy and complete this branching diagram, to show all the possible combinations of colour and model.

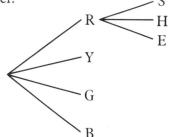

R ← S / H / E
Y
G
B

(b) Make a list of all the possible combinations. How many are there?

**B3** The new RX75 car comes in a choice of three colours: W (white), B (blue), O (orange).

There is a choice of two models: S (saloon), H (hatchback).

There is a choice of two engines: 1·3 litre, 1·6 litre

(a) Copy and complete the branching diagram.

(b) How many different possible combinations are there?

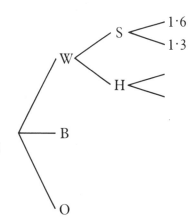

W < S < 1·6 / 1·3    H <
B
O

**B4** A club has to choose a chairman and a secretary.
There are five people to choose from: A, B, C, D and E.

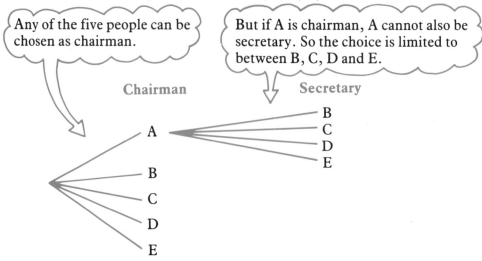

Any of the five people can be chosen as chairman.

But if A is chairman, A cannot also be secretary. So the choice is limited to between B, C, D and E.

(a) Copy the tree diagram and complete it.

(b) How many different ways are there to fill the two jobs?

**B5** A sports club has to choose a president and a vice-president.
There are six people to choose from: A, B, C and D are women and E and F are men.

The club has a rule that the president and vice-president cannot both be women or both be men.

Draw a tree diagram to show all the different ways to fill the jobs.

**B6** A political party has to choose a leader and a deputy leader.
There are four candidates for the leadership: A, B, C and D.
A and B are also candidates for the deputy leadership, but in addition there are two other candidates X and Y.

Draw a tree diagram to show all the different ways in which the two jobs can be filled. (The same person is not allowed to be both leader and deputy leader.)

**B7** Pupils at a school are going on a trip to London.

There are four places they can choose to visit: St Paul's, the Tower of London, the British Museum and the Science Museum.

Each pupil chooses one place to visit in the morning, and a different place to visit in the afternoon. The two places must not both be museums.

How many different ways can a pupil choose to spend the day?

B8  In a competition, entrants have to pick three features of a new car
    and put them in order of importance: 1st, 2nd, 3rd.

    The features they can choose from are

    A:  Safety belts on all seats          C:  Dual braking system
    B:  Rubber bumpers front and rear      D:  Economical engine

    (a) Copy and complete this tree diagram to show all the different
        possible entries.

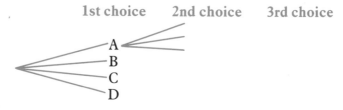

    (b) How many different possible entries are there?

## Permutations

A school Politics Club has invited three MPs to give talks at one of
its meetings. They are a Labour MP, a Liberal MP and a Conservative MP.

The club has to decide who is to speak first, who is to speak second and
who third.

Here are some of the possible orders of speaking.

    Lab, Lib, Con    Lib, Lab, Con    Con, Lib, Lab    Lab, Con, Lib

Each of these arrangements is called a **permutation** of the three speakers.

A permutation of a group of objects is a way of arranging them in
order: 1st, 2nd, 3rd, etc.

The permutations of a group of objects can be set out in a tree diagram.
Here is part of the tree diagram for the three speakers.

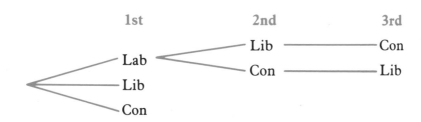

B9  (a) Copy and complete this tree diagram.

    (b) How many permutations of the three speakers are there?

## C Picture cards

The four cards on the opposite page come from a set of 24 cards.
They were made in Germany about a hundred years ago.

(The cards here have been lettered to make it easy to refer to them.)

The cards are designed so that any two of them placed side by side
will 'join up' to make a single picture.
This means that you can make many different pictures by rearranging
the cards.

For example, here are two of the different pictures you can make
starting with the lighthouse (card P) on the left.

**PQRS**

**PQSR**

C1 What other pictures could you make with the four cards starting
with card P on the left? Write them out using the letters.

C2 See how many pictures you can make starting with the rock (Q)
on the left.

C3 (a) How many different pictures can you make with the tree (R)
on the left?
(b) How many different pictures could be made altogether with
the four cards?

There are 24 cards in the full set. The number of different pictures you
could make using all 24 cards is over 620 000 000 000 000 000 000 000
($6.2 \times 10^{23}$).

P

*L. 12 L.*

Q

*U. 1 A.*

R

*L. 2. B.*

S

*K. 18. K.*

The cards on the opposite page come from another set made about 150 years ago.

They can be arranged in various ways to make different 'characters'.

C4 Here are 24 different characters which can be made from the cards on the opposite page. But there are three more possible characters that are not shown here.
See if you can work out which ones are missing.

# 7 Inverse proportionality

## A Inverse proportionality: introduction

Imagine that you are planning a journey of 120 miles.

On foot, going at **2 m.p.h.**, the journey would take **60 hours.**

At **3 m.p.h.**, it would take **40 hours.**

On a bike, going at **6 m.p.h.**, it would take **20 hours.**

By car, going at **30 m.p.h.**, it would take **4 hours.**

At **40 m.p.h.**, it would take **3 hours.**

At **60 m.p.h.**, it would take **2 hours.**

Here is a table of speed and journey times.

| Speed in m.p.h. | 2 | 3 | 6 | 30 | 40 | 60 |
|---|---|---|---|---|---|---|
| Journey time in hours | 60 | 40 | 20 | 4 | 3 | 2 |

Notice that

(1)  As the speed increases, so the journey time decreases.

(2)  If the speed is multiplied by 2, the time taken is divided by 2.

For example:

| | | $\xrightarrow{\times 2}$ | |
|---|---|---|---|
| **Speed** | 3 | | 6 |
| **Time** | 40 | | 20 |
| | | $\div 2$ | |

(3)  If the speed is multiplied by 3, the time taken is divided by 3.

For example:

| | | $\xrightarrow{\times 3}$ | |
|---|---|---|---|
| **Speed** | 2 | | 6 |
| **Time** | 60 | | 20 |
| | | $\div 3$ | |

(4)  If the speed is multiplied by 5, the time taken is divided by 5.

(Find an example of this in the table.)

We say that the journey time is **inversely proportional** to the speed.

If you multiply the speed by a number, then the journey time is divided by the same number.

**A1** A coach goes on a journey of 60 miles.

(a) Copy and complete this table of speeds and journey times.

| Speed in m.p.h. | 2 | 5 | 6 | 10 | 12 | 15 | 20 | 24 | 30 | 40 | 50 | 60 |
|---|---|---|---|---|---|---|---|---|---|---|---|---|
| Time in hours | | | | | | | | | | | | |

(b) Check that if the speed is multiplied by 3 (e.g. from 5 m.p.h. to 15 m.p.h.), the time is divided by 3.

(c) Check that if the speed is multiplied by 4, the time is divided by 4.

(d) Draw axes on graph paper. Use the scales shown here.

Plot the points from your table and draw a smooth curve through them.

(e) Let $s$ stand for the speed in m.p.h., and $t$ for the time in hours.

Write an equation connecting $s$ and $t$.

(Hint: Think about the value of $st$.)

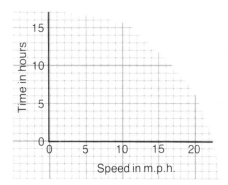

**A2** The time taken to cook a piece of meat in a microwave oven is inversely proportional to the power setting.

(a) If a piece of lamb will take 6 minutes on a power setting of 400 watts, how long will it take on a power setting of

(i) 800 watts   (ii) 200 watts   (iii) 100 watts   (iv) 300 watts

(b) Copy and complete this table of values using your answers to (a).

| Power in watts | 100 | 200 | 300 | 400 | 800 |
|---|---|---|---|---|---|
| Cooking time in minutes | | | | | |

(c) Draw a graph of (power, cooking time).

**A3** A piece of beef will take 4 minutes to cook on a power setting of 500 watts. Calculate the time it will take on a setting of 800 watts, like this:

(a) Calculate the multiplier from 500 watts to 800 watts.

(b) Divide by this number to find the new cooking time.

| | ×? | |
|---|---|---|
| **Power** | 500 | 800 |
| **Time** | 4 | |

## B  Mathematics and music

When a guitar string is plucked, it produces a musical note which
may be a high note or a low note. The highness or lowness depends on
the **frequency** with which the string vibrates.

Frequency is measured in **hertz** (Hz). A string which vibrates 200 times
per second produces a note whose frequency is **200 Hz**.

High notes have high frequencies and low notes low frequencies.

The frequency of the note produced by each string on a guitar depends on
how tight the string is, and on the length of the vibrating part of the string.

Before starting to play, the guitar player
adjusts the tightness of each string so
that it produces a certain note.

The player gets higher notes from the
same string by altering the length of the
vibrating part with his or her fingers.

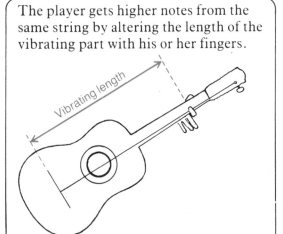

If the vibrating length is divided by 2, the frequency doubles (and we
hear the note 'an octave higher'). In fact, the frequency of the note
is **inversely proportional** to the length of the vibrating string.

### Worked example

A string of length 70 cm has been 'tuned' to produce a note whose frequency
is 110 Hz. Calculate the length which will produce a note of frequency 185 Hz.

First we work out the multiplier from
110 Hz to 185 Hz.

It is $\frac{185}{110} = 1 \cdot 68 \ldots$

The length is inversely proportional
to the frequency. So if the frequency is
multiplied by 1·68, the length has to
be **divided** by 1·68.

So the length has to be $\frac{70 \text{ cm}}{1 \cdot 68 \ldots} = 41 \cdot 6 \text{ cm}$

(to 3 s.f.)

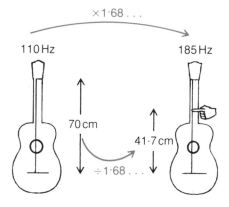

**B1** A string of length 65 cm has been tuned to produce a note whose frequency is 150 Hz. Calculate the length which will produce a note of frequency 175 Hz.

**B2** The note whose frequency is 110 Hz is called A. The second lowest string on a guitar is tuned to this note.

Here are the frequencies of some other notes which can be produced from the A-string, by altering the length.

| Note | B | C | D | E | F | G |
|---|---|---|---|---|---|---|
| Frequency | 124 | 131 | 147 | 165 | 175 | 196 |

If the vibrating A-string (110 Hz) is 70 cm long, calculate the length needed to produce each of the notes in the table.

**B3** Another string on a guitar is tuned to the note D (147 Hz). If this string is 70 cm long, calculate the length of it which will produce the note G (196 Hz).

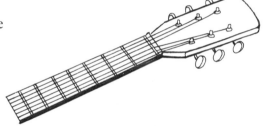

On a guitar there are 'frets' which enable the player to get the right length of string for each note.

The spacing of these frets is worked out from calculations like those you have just done in questions B2 and B3.

**Facts about frequencies**

This diagram shows the frequencies of some of the notes on a piano. (They are all As.)

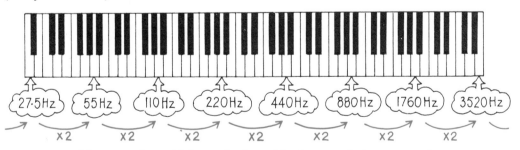

The range of frequencies which can be heard by human beings extends from about 15 Hz to 20 000 Hz, but the upper limit comes down as people get older. Dogs and cats can hear frequencies up to 60 000 Hz, and bats up to 80 000 Hz.

## c  Direct and inverse proportionality

Here are some of the differences between direct and inverse proportionality.

---

**Direct proportionality**

Example: The cost of petrol is directly proportional to the quantity you buy.

If you multiply the quantity by a number, then you multiply the cost by the same number

The graph of (quantity, cost) is a straight line going through $(0, 0)$.

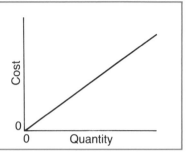

---

**Inverse proportionality**

Example: The time taken to cook a joint in a microwave oven is inversely proportional to the power setting.

If you multiply the power by a number, then you divide the time by the same number.

The graph of (power, time) is a curve. As the power increases, so the time decreases.

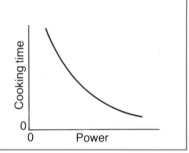

---

There are many examples of both kinds of proportionality in science.

**C1** The electrical resistance of copper wire of uniform thickness is directly proportional to the length of the wire.

A wire 600 cm long has a resistance of 33·0 ohms. Calculate the resistance of (a) 900 cm  (b) 250 cm of the wire.

**C2** Boyle's law says that the volume of some enclosed gas is inversely proportional to its pressure.

(For example, doubling the pressure will halve the volume.)

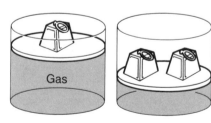

Suppose that when the pressure is 800 millibars, the volume is 18 litres.

Calculate the volume when the pressure is

(a)  400 millibars       (b)  1200 millibars

(c)  600 millibars       (d)  1000 millibars

# 8 Using algebra

## A Finding and stating rules

### A1 Crosses

This cross is made from square tiles.

Each 'arm' of the cross is 3 squares long. There are 13 squares altogether in the cross.

(a) Imagine a similar cross with 5 squares in each arm. What is the total number of squares in the cross?

(b) Let $n$ stand for the number of squares in each arm of a cross.

Write down a formula for the total number of squares in the cross.

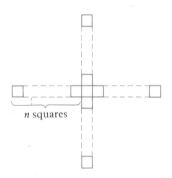

$n$ squares

### A2 Tables and chairs (1)

The owner of a café arranges square tables in rows, like this:

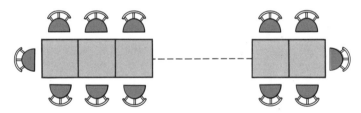

(a) If there are 9 tables in a row, how many chairs will be needed to go with them?

(b) How many chairs will be needed to go with a row of 50 tables?

(c) Imagine a row of tables, and let the number of tables in the row be $n$.

Find a formula for the number of chairs which will be needed to go with $n$ tables.

Choose a value for $n$ (say 7) and check that your formula gives the correct result.

## A3 Tables and chairs (2)

Another café owner has rectangular tables, which she arranges in rows like this:

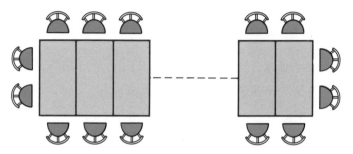

Find a formula for the number of chairs needed to go with a row of $n$ tables.

## A4 Tables and chairs (3)

The second café owner could also arrange her tables in rows like this:

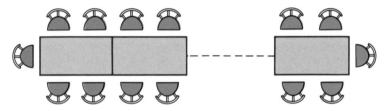

Find a formula for the number of chairs needed when there are $n$ tables in a row.

## A5 Squares and triangles

Look at these arrangements of squares and triangles.

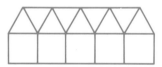

5 squares, 9 triangles

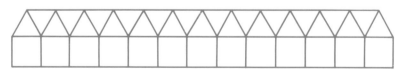

13 squares, 25 triangles

Find a formula for the number of triangles needed when there are $n$ squares.

## A6 Fences

This fence has 5 posts and 8 bars.

Imagine a similar fence with $n$ posts.
Find a formula for the number of bars it will have.

## A7 Matches (1)

This row of squares is made with matches.

To make 4 squares, you need 13 matches.

Find a formula for the number of matches needed to make $n$ squares in a row.

## A8 Matches (2)

Find a formula for the number of matches needed to make $n$ rectangles in a row

(a) like this

. . . and so on

(b) like this

. . . and so on

# B Translating into algebra

Algebra is a language which we can use to state relationships **clearly** and **concisely** (briefly).

For example, we can translate this:

'To find the perimeter of a rectangle, add together the length and the width and then multiply the result by 2.'

into algebra like this:

'Let $P$ be the perimeter of a rectangle, $l$ the length and $w$ the width. Then $P = 2(l + w)$.'

B1 'To calculate the mean of three numbers, add them together and divide the result by 3.'
Let $m$ be the mean and $a$, $b$ and $c$ the three numbers.
Translate the rule above into algebra.

**B2** 'To calculate the area of an equilateral triangle, multiply the length of a side by itself and multiply the result by 0·866.'

Let $A$ be the area and $s$ the length of a side. Translate the rule above into algebra.

**B3** 'To calculate the time in seconds for one complete swing (to and fro) of a simple pendulum, take the square root of the length in metres of the pendulum and double it.'

Translate this rule into algebra, using $T$ to stand for the time in seconds for a complete swing and $l$ for the length in metres.

**B4** Let $w$ stand for the weight of a mouse and $f$ for the weight of the food it eats in one day.

Translate into algebra: 'A mouse eats the equivalent of half of its own weight in food each day.'

**B5** Plumbers often divide the charge they make into two parts:
(1) a fixed 'call-out' charge which the customer has to pay, no matter how long the job takes to do;
(2) a charge per hour for the work done.

(a) Calculate the total cost of a job if the fixed charge is £5, the hourly rate is £13 per hour and the job takes 5 hours to do.

(b) Let £$F$ stand for a plumber's fixed charge, £$R$ for the rate per hour, $T$ for the number of hours and £$C$ for the total cost.

Write a formula which explains how to work out $C$ when you know $F$, $R$ and $T$.

**B6** If a widow dies, leaving an amount of money but no will, any outstanding debts and estate duty are first paid out and what remains is divided equally between the widow's children (if she has any).

Let £$L$ stand for the amount the widow leaves, £$D$ for the total of outstanding debts and estate duty, and $n$ for the number of children. Let £$S$ stand for each child's share.

Write a formula which explains how to calculate $S$ given $L$, $D$ and $n$.

**B7** A shelf of length $s$ cm is mounted on a wall of length $w$ cm, so that the gaps at each end are equal.

If the width of each gap is $g$ cm, find a formula which explains how to calculate $g$ when you know $s$ and $w$.

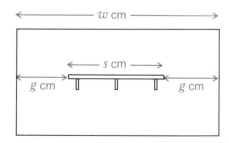

# C Making use of formulas

When a relationship has been translated into algebra as a formula, the formula can be used to solve different kinds of problem.

**Worked example**

Use the formula $P = 2(l + w)$ to find $w$ when $P = 216$ and $l = 51$.

Substitute the known values into the formula: $216 = 2(51 + w)$

Divide both sides by 2. $108 = 51 + w$

Subtract 51 from both sides. $57 = w$

**C1** In the worked example we solved the equation $216 = 2(51 \times w)$ by first dividing both sides by 2.
Another way is first to multiply out the brackets. Do this and finish solving the equation.

**C2** Re-arrange the formula $P = 2(l + w)$ to make $w$ the subject.

**C3** If $m$ is the number of matches needed to make a row of $n$ rectangles like this, then

$$m = 5n + 1.$$

... etc.

(a) Calculate $n$ given that $m = 86$.

(b) Re-arrange the formula to make $n$ the subject.

**C4** If $b$ is the number of bars needed to make a fence like this with $n$ posts, then

 ... etc.

$$b = 3\,(n - 1).$$

(a) Calculate $n$ given that $b = 78$.

(b) Re-arrange the formula to make $n$ the subject.

**C5** Re-arrange each of these formulas to make the letter printed in red the subject.

(a) $y = 3x + 5$      (b) $y = ax + b$

(c) $s = 3q - r$      (d) $s = pq - r$

(e) $h = 8 - g$      (f) $h = 9 - 2g$

(g) $h = a - 5g$      (h) $h = a - bg$

(i) $z = \dfrac{x}{2y}$      (j) $v = \dfrac{a}{2u}$

# 9 Trigonometry (3)

## A The sine of an angle

The picture on the right shows an escalator. The sloping section is 12 metres long. It slopes at an angle of 35° to the horizontal.

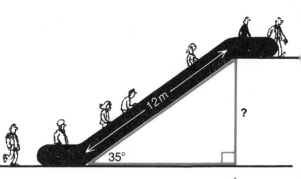

The problem is to find how high the top of the escalator is above the bottom.

This may remind you of the type of problem where you use the tangent of the angle. But the tangent is used when you are dealing with the side **adjacent** to the angle and the side **opposite** the angle.

What we are given here is the **hypotenuse**.

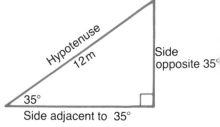

In a right-angled triangle with an angle θ in it,

the ratio $\dfrac{\text{side opposite } \theta}{\text{hypotenuse}}$ is called the **sine** of θ,

written **sin θ** (but pronounced sine θ).

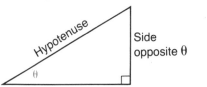

To calculate the side opposite θ, you multiply the hypotenuse by sin θ.

$$\text{hyp} \times \sin \theta = \text{opp}$$

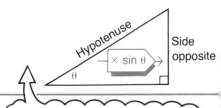

You may find it helpful to copy this diagram and formula into your book.

Here is a table of the sines of some angles, to 3 decimal places.

| θ | 0° | 5° | 10° | 15° | 20° | 25° | 30° | 35° | 40° | 45° |
|---|---|---|---|---|---|---|---|---|---|---|
| sin θ | 0 | 0·087 | 0·174 | 0·259 | 0·342 | 0·423 | 0·500 | 0·574 | 0·643 | 0·707 |

| θ | 50° | ·55° | 60° | 65° | 70° | 75° | 80° | 85° | 90° |
|---|---|---|---|---|---|---|---|---|---|
| sin θ | 0·766 | 0·819 | 0·866 | 0·906 | 0·940 | 0·966 | 0·985 | 0·996 | 1 |

In the case of the escalator on the opposite page, the hypotenuse is 12 m and the angle is 35°.

So 12 × sin 35° = side opposite 35°.

From the table of sines, sin 35° = 0·574, so 12 × 0·574 = side opposite 35°.

So the side opposite 35° is **6·9 m** (to 1 d.p.), and this is the height of the top of the escalator above the bottom.

**A1** Calculate the lengths marked with letters in these triangles. Use the table of sines on the previous page. Give answers to 1 d.p.

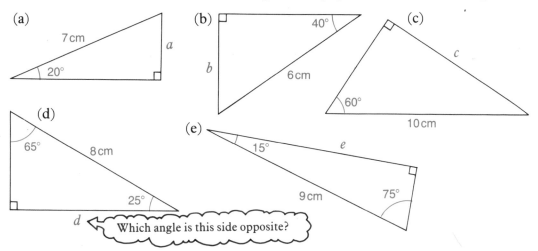
(a) 7 cm, 20°, *a*
(b) *b*
(c) 40°, 6 cm, 60°, *c*, 10 cm

(d) 65°, 8 cm, 25°, *d* — Which angle is this side opposite?
(e) 15°, *e*, 9 cm, 75°

## Using a calculator

To find sin 40° on a calculator, enter 40 first and then press ⟨sin⟩ .

To work out 12 × sin 40°, on most calculators you do this:

Enter 12 ⟶ Press ⟨×⟩ ⟶ Enter 40 ⟶ Press ⟨sin⟩ ⟶ Press ⟨=⟩

**A2** Calculate the lengths marked with letters, correct to 1 d.p.

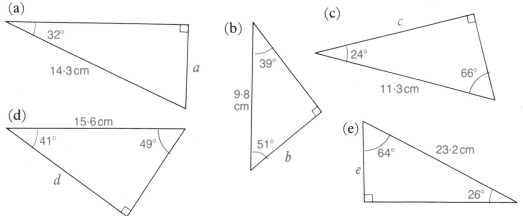
(a) 32°, 14·3 cm
(b) 39°, 9·8 cm, *a*, 51°, *b*
(c) *c*, 24°, 11·3 cm, 66°
(d) 15·6 cm, 41°, 49°, *d*
(e) 64°, *e*, 23·2 cm, 26°

This page has a mixture of problems on it.
Some of them require **sines** and some **tangents**.
As a reminder, here are the basic 'tangent' diagram
and formula.

$$\text{adj} \times \tan \theta = \text{opp}$$

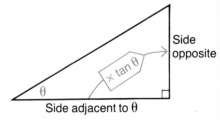

**A3**  Make a sketch of each triangle, and label its sides 'hyp' (hypotenuse),
'opp' (opposite the given angle) and 'adj' (adjacent to the given angle).
Decide whether to use sine or tangent to calculate the length asked for.

Give each answer correct to 1 decimal place.

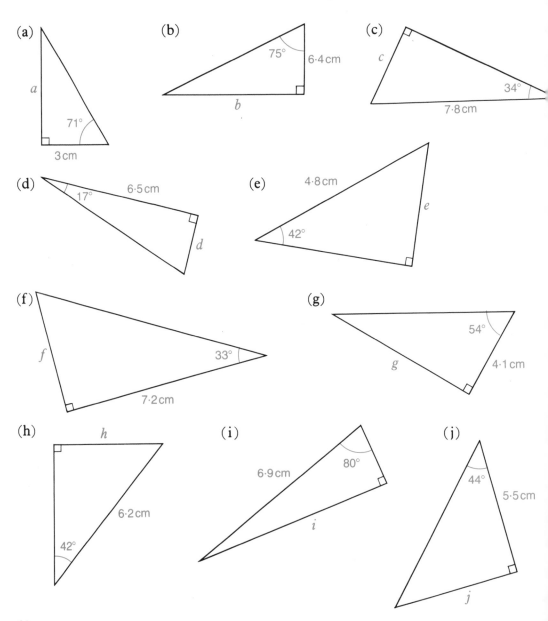

## B  The cosine of an angle

The cosine is another ratio which is useful for calculating
sides of right-angled triangles.

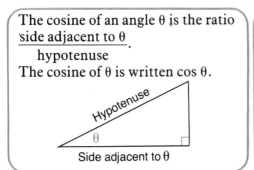

The cosine of an angle θ is the ratio
$\dfrac{\text{side adjacent to } \theta}{\text{hypotenuse}}$.

The cosine of θ is written cos θ.

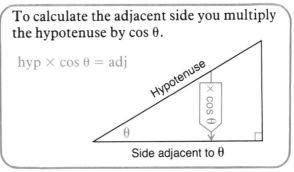

To calculate the adjacent side you multiply
the hypotenuse by cos θ.

$$\text{hyp} \times \cos \theta = \text{adj}$$

### Worked example

Calculate the side marked $x$ in this triangle.

The sides are labelled 'hyp', 'opp' and 'adj'.

We need to use the formula

$$\text{hyp} \times \cos \theta = \text{adj}$$

So $8 \cdot 5 \times \cos 64° = \text{adj}$

On a calculator we do $\boxed{8}\,\boxed{\cdot}\,\boxed{5}\,\boxed{\times}\,\boxed{6}\,\boxed{4}\,\boxed{\cos}\,\boxed{=}$   and get **$3 \cdot 7\,\text{cm}$** (to 1 d.p.).

**B1**  Calculate the lengths marked with letters, to 1 d.p.

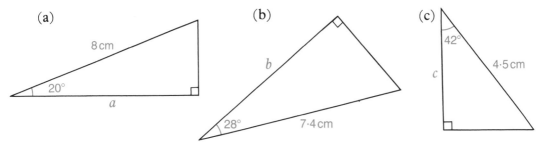

(a)

8 cm

20°

$a$

(b)

$b$

28°          7·4 cm

(c)

42°

4·5 cm

$c$

**B2**  A ladder which is 6·4 m long leans
against a vertical wall and makes
an angle of 67° with the ground.
Calculate, to the nearest 0·1 m, how
far the bottom of the ladder is from
the wall.

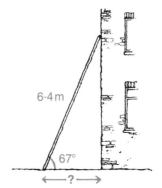

6·4 m

67°

←—?—→

**B3** Calculate the width (marked $w$) of the building in this diagram.

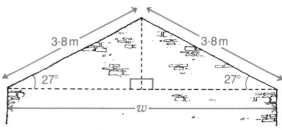

## C Calculating sides

We now know three formulas connecting sides and angles of a right-angled triangle.

$$\text{adj} \times \tan \theta = \text{opp}$$

$$\text{hyp} \times \sin \theta = \text{opp}$$

$$\text{hyp} \times \cos \theta = \text{adj}$$

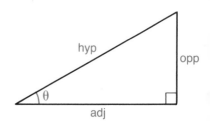

Here is a good method to follow when you have to calculate one of the sides of a right-angled triangle, given an angle.

**1** Label the sides:
hyp   (hypotenuse)
opp   (opposite the given angle)
adj   (adjacent to the given angle)

**2** Choose the formula which contains both the **side you know** and the **side you want** to calculate.
Write down that formula.

For example, suppose you want to calculate the side marked $x$ in this triangle.

Label the three sides 'hyp', 'opp' and 'adj'.

The formula which contains the side you know (7·6) and the side you want ($x$) is

$$\text{hyp} \times \sin \theta = \text{opp}$$

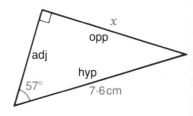

**C1** Calculate the lengths marked with letters, to 1 d.p.

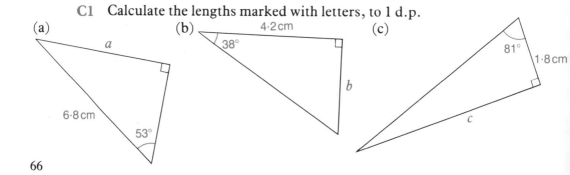

(a)

(b)

(c)

**C2** Calculate the lengths marked with letters, to 1 d.p.

(a)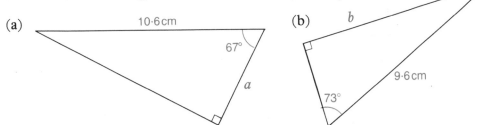

10·6 cm

67°

a

(b)

b

9·6 cm

73°

**C3** Calculate the heights of the points A, B, C above the ground, each to the nearest 0·1 m.

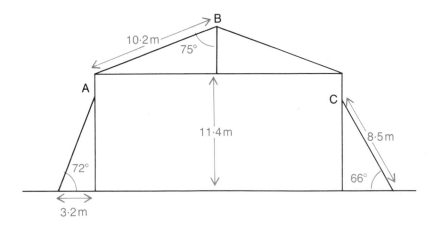

B

10·2 m

75°

A

11·4 m

C

8·5 m

72°

66°

3·2 m

**C4** Calculate the lengths marked a and b in this right-angled triangle.

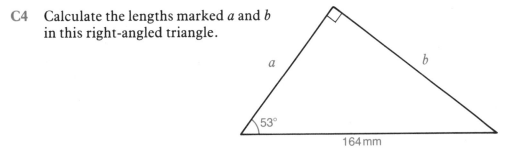

a

b

53°

164 mm

**C5** Calculate the length of (a) BD (b) DC in the diagram below.

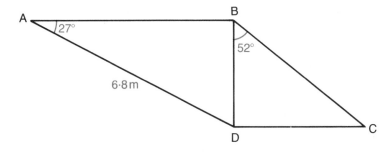

A

27°

B

52°

6·8 m

D

C

Sometimes when you put the values you know into the formula you end up with an equation to solve.

**Worked example**

Calculate the length marked $p$ in this triangle.

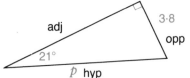

Here we know 'opp' and have to calculate 'hyp', so the formula to use is
hyp $\times \sin \theta = $ opp.

So    $p \times \sin 21° = 3{\cdot}8$.

So    $p = \dfrac{3{\cdot}8}{\sin 21°} = 10{\cdot}6\,\text{cm (to 1 d.p.).}$

C6  Calculate the lettered sides of these triangles, to the nearest $0{\cdot}1\,\text{cm}$.

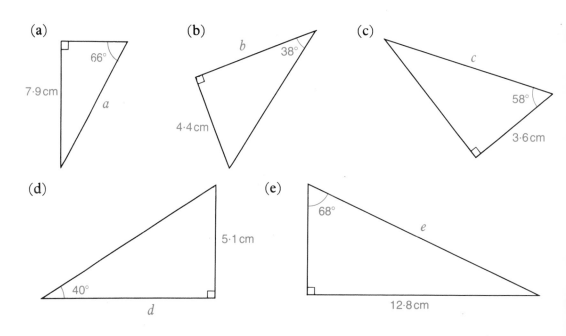

(a)

66°

7·9 cm

$a$

(b)

$b$

38°

4·4 cm

(c)

$c$

58°

3·6 cm

(d)

40°

$d$

5·1 cm

(e)

68°

$e$

12·8 cm

Some of the questions which follow are straightforward applications of the three basic formulas. In others you will get an equation to solve.

C7  Calculate

(a) BD

(b) DC

in this diagram.

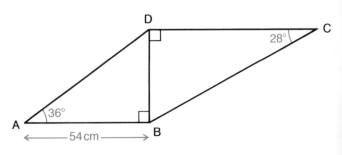

D

28°

C

36°

A

54 cm

B

**C8** Calculate the length of

(a) PQ

(b) PS

in this diagram.

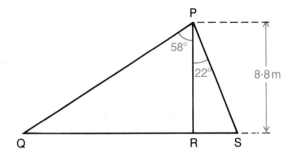

**C9** Calculate the length of (a) AB (b) BC (c) AC in this diagram.

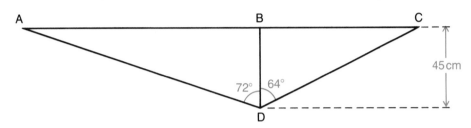

**C10** UV and XY are two vertical mine shafts, and VY is a tunnel.

Calculate the length VY.

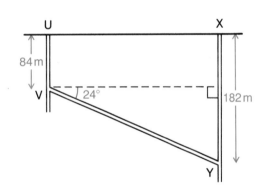

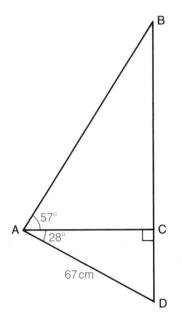

**C11** Calculate

(a) AC

(b) AB

in the diagram on the left.

# 10 Graphs and charts

## A Bar charts

Tuberculosis is a very serious disease, usually affecting the lungs. It is much less common now than it was in the past, thanks largely to vaccination.

This table shows the number of cases of tuberculosis in Britain in various years.

| Year | 1921 | 1931 | 1941 | 1951 | 1961 | 1971 |
|---|---|---|---|---|---|---|
| Number of cases | 85 000 | 83 000 | 70 000 | 60 000 | 26 000 | 13 000 |

Most people find it easier to 'take in' information like this if it is presented in the form of a picture.

Here is a **bar chart** which shows the information.

You can see very clearly the huge drop in the number of cases between 1951 and 1961. (The BCG vaccination was introduced in 1954.)

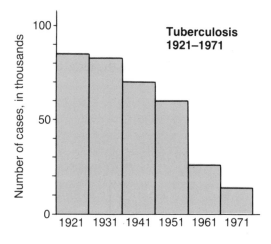

A line graph can also be used to show the same information.

The dotted lines on this graph are there just to help the eye. You cannot use this graph to find the number of cases between the years given.

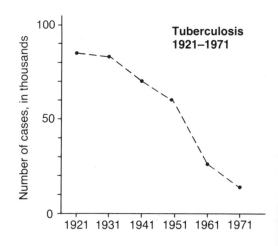

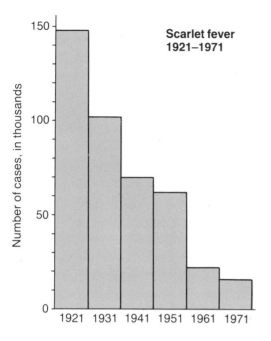

**Scarlet fever 1921–1971**

Number of cases, in thousands

**A1** This bar chart shows how the number of cases of scarlet fever dropped between 1921 and 1971.

(a) Estimate from the chart the number of cases in 1921.

(b) Estimate the number of cases in 1931.

(c) Estimate the number of cases in 1971.

We can estimate percentage decreases (and increases) from a bar chart.

Here for example are the bars for 1931 and 1941 from the chart above.

We imagine the 1931 bar split into 10 equal parts. Each part is 10% of the 1931 bar.

We can see that the 1941 bar is about 70% of the 1931 bar.
So there was a **30% decrease** in scarlet fever cases between 1931 and 1941.

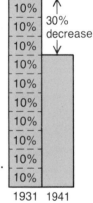

**A2** Estimate from the chart above the percentage decrease in scarlet fever cases between 1921 and 1931. (Estimate to the nearest 10%.)

**A3** Estimate to the nearest 10% the percentage decrease in scarlet fever cases between

(a) 1941 and 1951    (b) 1951 and 1961

**A4** Use the chart on the opposite page to estimate the percentage drop in the number of cases of tuberculosis between 1951 and 1961.

**A5** Use the figures in the table on the opposite page to calculate the percentage drop in tuberculosis cases between 1951 and 1961, to the nearest 10%.

The diagram below consists of two bar charts put together.
One bar chart shows the populations of the major urban regions of England.
The other shows their areas.

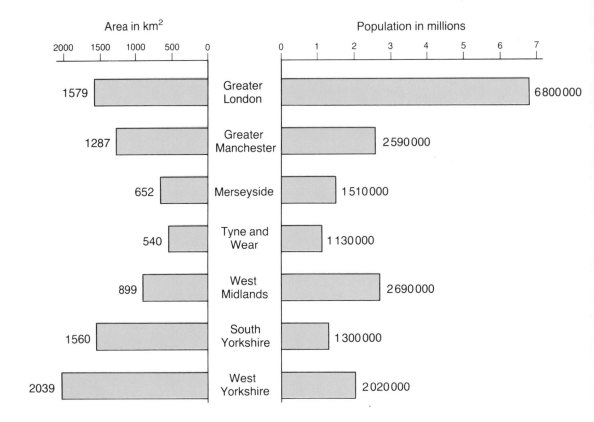

Major urban regions of England

A6 (a) Which of the regions in the chart has the largest population?

(b) Which has the smallest area?

From the chart you will see that Greater Manchester and the West Midlands
have roughly the same population, but the area of the West Midlands is
quite a bit smaller.

We can compare these two regions by calculating their **population densities**,
which are measured in **people per square kilometre**.
To do this, we divide a region's population by its area.

The population density of Greater Manchester is $\frac{2\,590\,000}{1287} = 2012$ people per km$^2$
(to the nearest whole number)

So, in Greater Manchester, there are 2012 people for each square kilometre
of space.

**A7** Calculate the population density of the West Midlands, and compare it with that for Greater Manchester.

**A8** (a) Calculate the population densities of the other regions in the chart. Make a table of population densities, showing the seven regions in order of population density, highest first.

(b) Draw a bar chart to show this information.

**A9** This chart gives information about eight English counties.

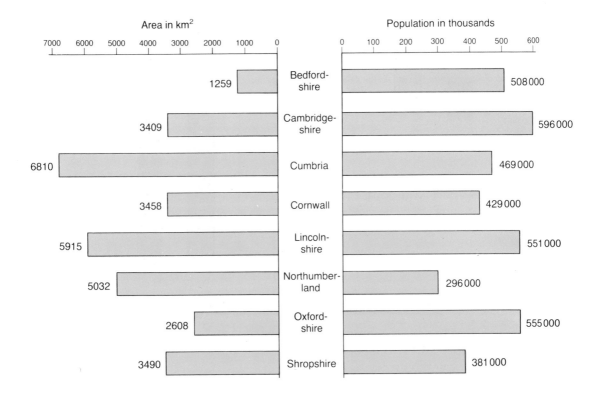

(a) Without doing any calculations, can you pick out the county which is most densely populated? It is the one whose population is the largest **in relation to its area**.

(b) Can you pick out the county which is least densely populated?

(c) Calculate the population density of each of the eight counties, and arrange the counties in order with the most densely populated first.

## B  Misleading charts

Sometimes people use charts to mislead others.

When you look quickly at this chart, it looks as if this month's sales are about double last month's.

When you look at the scale at the side of the chart, you can see that it does not start at 0.

If the whole chart is drawn, it looks like this. Sales have increased, but **not** doubled.

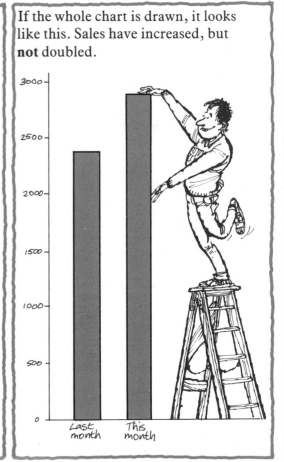

If you draw a bar chart whose scale does not start at 0, it is better to draw broken bars, like this. (Unless, of course, you want to mislead!)

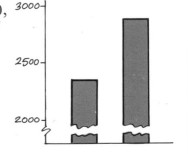

**B1**  This chart shows a firm's profits in 1986 and 1987.

Why is the chart misleading?

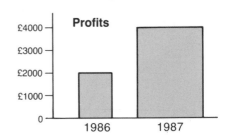

Charts are often made to look more like pictures.
Sometimes the pictures can be misleading.

**B2** A bakery increased its sales of loaves from 300 000 in November to 900 000 in December. So the December sales were 3 times the November sales.

Which of these two charts gives a fairer picture of the increase, and why?

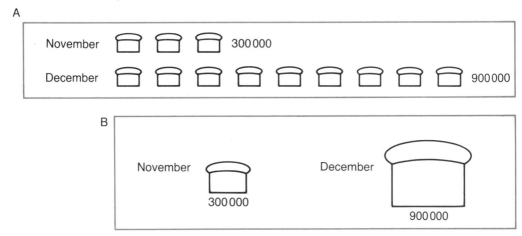

A

November ⌂ ⌂ ⌂ 300 000

December ⌂ ⌂ ⌂ ⌂ ⌂ ⌂ ⌂ ⌂ ⌂ 900 000

B

November ⌂ 300 000

December ⌂ 900 000

**B3**

This photo was taken during the 1983 election campaign.
It shows the Minister of Health and Social Security with charts showing increases in spending on the National Health Service.
Do the charts give a fair picture of the figures?

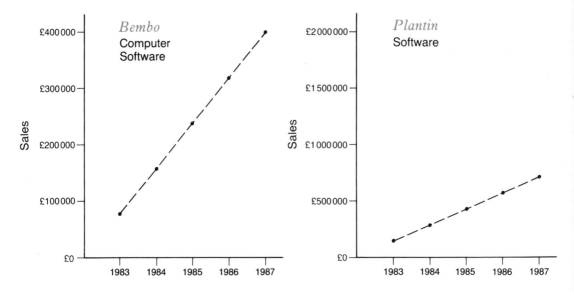

**B4** Look at the two graphs above.
Which of the two businesses is growing faster?

**B5** Why is the graph below misleading?

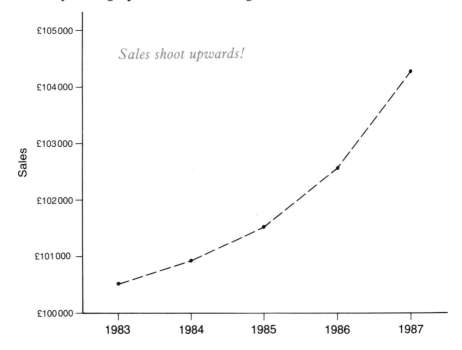

**B6** Imagine that you own a business. Your sales figures for the past
five years have been £20 000, £25 000, £28 000, £27 000, £27 500.

Draw a chart which shows how well you have done. You don't
have to use all the figures.

# 11 Vectors

## A  Column vectors

An insect moves from the point A to the
point B in this diagram.

We can describe its movement by using
two numbers, like this.

The number of units it moves **across**.

The number of units it moves **up**.

We write the two numbers one above the other, in brackets.

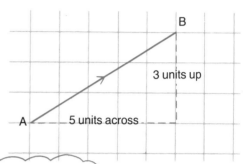

3 units up

A ———— 5 units across ————

The arrow from A to B is called a **vector**. It is written $\overrightarrow{AB}$.

$\overrightarrow{AB}$ is '5 units across, 3 units up', so we write $\overrightarrow{AB} = \begin{bmatrix} 5 \\ 3 \end{bmatrix}$.

$\begin{bmatrix} 5 \\ 3 \end{bmatrix}$ is called a **column vector**. (The two numbers are written in a column.)

A1  Write down the column vector of each of these vectors.

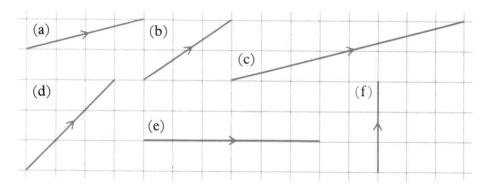

(a)     (b)

(c)

(d)     (f)

(e)

A2  Look at the vector $\overrightarrow{PQ}$ in
    this diagram.

    You **cannot** call it $\begin{bmatrix} 3 \\ 4 \end{bmatrix}$

    because $\begin{bmatrix} 3 \\ 4 \end{bmatrix}$ slopes upwards.

    How would you write the
    column vector of $\overrightarrow{PQ}$?

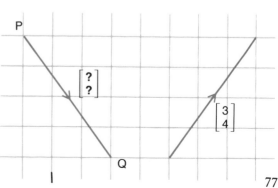

77

From P to Q is 3 units to the right and 4 units **down**.

We write it $\begin{bmatrix} 3 \\ -4 \end{bmatrix}$.

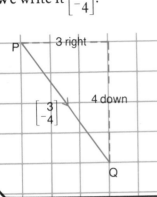

Here is another vector which needs a negative number.

It is 3 units to the **left** and 2 units up.

We write it $\begin{bmatrix} -3 \\ 2 \end{bmatrix}$.

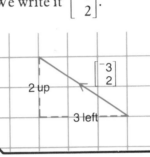

This vector needs two negative numbers.

It is 3 units to the **left** and 2 units **down**.

We write it $\begin{bmatrix} -3 \\ -2 \end{bmatrix}$.

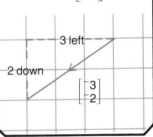

**A3** Write down the column vector of each of these vectors.

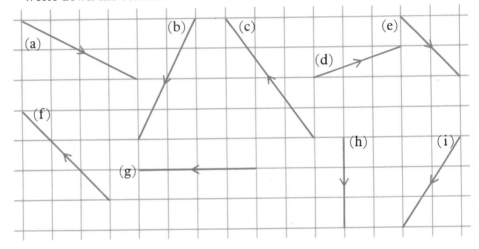

**A4** A marker moves from A to B like this.

The first vector is $\begin{bmatrix} 3 \\ 1 \end{bmatrix}$.

(a) What are the other two vectors?

(b) If you start at A and use the three vectors in a different order, like this, $\begin{bmatrix} 0 \\ 3 \end{bmatrix}$, $\begin{bmatrix} 2 \\ 3 \end{bmatrix}$, $\begin{bmatrix} 3 \\ 1 \end{bmatrix}$, where do you finish?

(c) Do you always finish at B, no matter what order you use the three vectors?

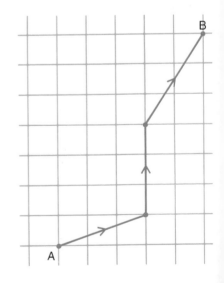

78

A5 Mark a point P on a grid.

(a) A marker starts at P and moves along these three vectors in order:
$\begin{bmatrix} 3 \\ 1 \end{bmatrix}$, $\begin{bmatrix} -2 \\ 3 \end{bmatrix}$, $\begin{bmatrix} 5 \\ -1 \end{bmatrix}$.

Draw its journey. Mark the finishing point Q.

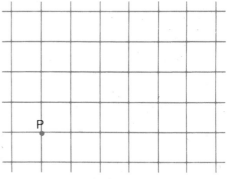

(b) The marker starts again at P. This time it moves along the vectors in the order $\begin{bmatrix} 5 \\ -1 \end{bmatrix}$, $\begin{bmatrix} 3 \\ 1 \end{bmatrix}$, $\begin{bmatrix} -2 \\ 3 \end{bmatrix}$. Draw its journey.

(c) The marker starts again at P. It moves along the vectors in this order: $\begin{bmatrix} -2 \\ 3 \end{bmatrix}$, $\begin{bmatrix} 5 \\ -1 \end{bmatrix}$, $\begin{bmatrix} 3 \\ 1 \end{bmatrix}$. Draw its journey.

A6 You want to get from A to B. You can use **two** of these four vectors:

$\begin{bmatrix} 1 \\ -2 \end{bmatrix}$, $\begin{bmatrix} 3 \\ 2 \end{bmatrix}$, $\begin{bmatrix} 4 \\ -1 \end{bmatrix}$, $\begin{bmatrix} 2 \\ -3 \end{bmatrix}$.

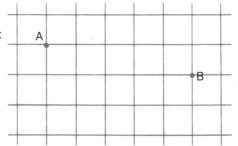

(a) Which two vectors do you need?

(b) Does it matter which order you use them?

A7 You can get from A to B in the diagram above by using **three** of these five vectors. Which three do you need?

$\begin{bmatrix} -1 \\ -2 \end{bmatrix}$, $\begin{bmatrix} 3 \\ 1 \end{bmatrix}$, $\begin{bmatrix} -1 \\ 1 \end{bmatrix}$, $\begin{bmatrix} -2 \\ -2 \end{bmatrix}$, $\begin{bmatrix} 7 \\ 0 \end{bmatrix}$

A8 **A vector code**

Start at the point marked T.

Each vector in the list below takes you from letter to letter.

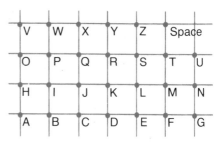

$\begin{bmatrix} -5 \\ -1 \end{bmatrix}$ $\begin{bmatrix} 1 \\ 0 \end{bmatrix}$ $\begin{bmatrix} 3 \\ 1 \end{bmatrix}$ $\begin{bmatrix} 1 \\ 1 \end{bmatrix}$ $\begin{bmatrix} -4 \\ -2 \end{bmatrix}$ $\begin{bmatrix} 3 \\ 1 \end{bmatrix}$ $\begin{bmatrix} 1 \\ 1 \end{bmatrix}$ $\begin{bmatrix} -5 \\ -3 \end{bmatrix}$ $\begin{bmatrix} 6 \\ 1 \end{bmatrix}$ $\begin{bmatrix} -1 \\ 2 \end{bmatrix}$ $\begin{bmatrix} -1 \\ -3 \end{bmatrix}$ $\begin{bmatrix} -4 \\ 0 \end{bmatrix}$ $\begin{bmatrix} 4 \\ 2 \end{bmatrix}$ $\begin{bmatrix} -1 \\ 1 \end{bmatrix}$

$\begin{bmatrix} 2 \\ 0 \end{bmatrix}$ $\begin{bmatrix} 0 \\ -1 \end{bmatrix}$ $\begin{bmatrix} -5 \\ -2 \end{bmatrix}$ $\begin{bmatrix} 4 \\ 2 \end{bmatrix}$ $\begin{bmatrix} -1 \\ -1 \end{bmatrix}$

## B  Translations

The girl in this picture is about to move the table.

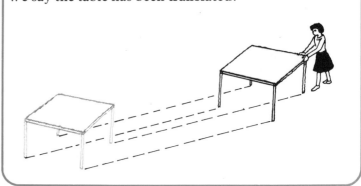

She drags it across the floor without rotating it. We say the table has been **translated**.

We can use a column vector to describe a translation.

In this diagram every point of the table moves along a vector $\begin{bmatrix} 6 \\ 3 \end{bmatrix}$.

$\begin{bmatrix} 6 \\ 3 \end{bmatrix}$ is the column vector of the translation.

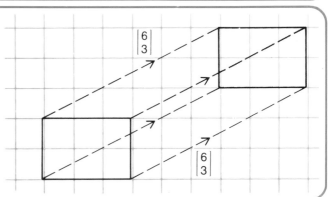

B1  The left-hand set of points is translated onto the right-hand set.

What is the column vector of the translation?

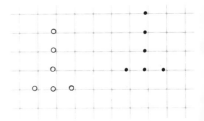

B2  Sam said that the column vector of the translation from shape A to shape B is $\begin{bmatrix} 3 \\ 2 \end{bmatrix}$.

He is wrong. What is the column vector of the translation?

80

**B3** Copy this diagram on squared paper.
Translate the shape using the column
vector $\begin{bmatrix} 4 \\ -1 \end{bmatrix}$.

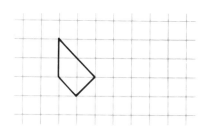

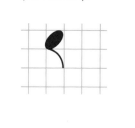

**B4** Write down the column vector of
each of these translations.

(a) A to B     (b) A to C

(c) A to F     (d) E to A

(e) B to E     (f) G to E

(g) C to E     (h) E to C

(i) D to E     (j) B to A

## Repeating patterns

Translations are used to make repeating patterns.

**1**   Start with a design
(or 'motif').

**2**   Translate the design, using the same vector again
and again. Continue the pattern 'backwards',
to get an infinite **strip pattern**.

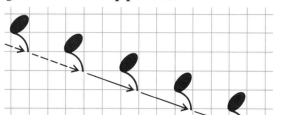

**3**   Choose a different vector.
Translate the whole strip
pattern again and again.
Continue backwards.

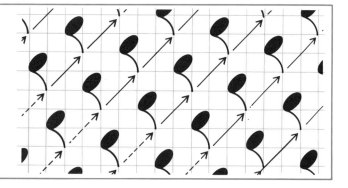

# Money matters : Insurance

## Holiday medical insurance

If you go abroad for a holiday, you may fall ill or have an accident, and need medical treatment.

Medical treatment is often expensive abroad.

So it is a good idea to **insure** yourself against medical expenses.

To do this, you pay a fairly small amount of money, called a **premium**, to an insurance company. The company then agrees to pay any medical expenses which may arise on your holiday, up to a certain amount.

Here for example are the premiums charged by the 'Globule Insurance Co.' for different lengths of holiday.

| Globule Insurance | | 10 days | 20 days | 30 days |
|---|---|---|---|---|
| Medical | £1000 | £1·50 | £2·75 | £4·00 |
| expenses | £5000 | £5·00 | £8·50 | £11·50 |
| up to | £10 000 | £8·00 | £14·50 | £19·50 |

Why is the insurance company willing to do this? They know, from past experience, that most holidaymakers do not fall ill or have accidents on holiday. So most of the people who pay their premiums will not need to have medical expenses paid for them.

The company tries to fix the premiums so that it can pay the expenses of the few people who do need treatment out of the total of all the premiums paid in. It also makes sure that there is enough left over to pay the costs of running the business, and make a profit.

Insurance companies know from experience that in some parts of the world a holidaymaker is more likely to need medical treatment than in others. So the premiums for these places are higher.

1 Insurance companies generally have higher premiums for winter sports holidays than for summer holidays. Why is this?

# Car and motorcycle insurance

Motorcyclists and car drivers are required by law to be insured.
There are three main types of insurance they can have.

(1) **Third party.** If the driver (or rider) is involved in an accident in which another person is injured or killed or another vehicle damaged, the insurance company pays any compensation, and the cost of any repairs to the other vehicle.

(2) **Third party, fire and theft.** The insurance company also pays if the driver's own vehicle is damaged by fire or stolen.

(3) **Comprehensive.** The company also pays for the repairs to the driver's own vehicle if it is damaged in an accident.

The premium which the driver pays depends on a number of things:
the type of insurance; the driver's age and occupation; where the driver lives; the make, model and age of the car or motorbike.

Different companies have different premiums, so it is a good idea to shop around to get the best deal.

The premium covers one year's insurance. If the insurance company does not have to pay out anything during that year, then it usually gives the driver a **no claims discount** on his or her next year's premium.
Here is an example of the 'no claims discounts' offered by one company.

| | |
|---|---|
| 1 year's claim-free insurance | 25% discount |
| 2 years' claim-free insurance | 40% discount |
| 3 years' claim-free insurance | 50% discount |
| 4 or more years' claim-free insurance | 60% discount |

This means the driver pays 25% less than the normal premium.

If the company has to pay out during a year's insurance, the driver loses two years' discount. (So 60% discount becomes 40%, 50% becomes 25%.)

2 Janice is 22 years old, lives in Birmingham and drives an 8 year old Ford Escort 1300.

In her first year of driving she was comprehensively insured and paid the normal premium of £180.

She is a very careful driver, and she made no claim during that year (so the insurance company did not have to pay out anything). So she was allowed a 25% no claims discount on her premium for the second year.

(a) If the normal premium was still £180, what did Janice have to pay in her second year?

(b) Janice made no claim during her second year and she is now going to insure for her third year. The insurance company allows her a 40% no claims discount. The company has increased all its premiums, so the normal premium is now £210. What will Janice have to pay?

# 6 Arranging and selecting (2)

6.1 Suppose you have three rubber stamps, for printing the figures 1, 2 and 3.

What different three-figure numbers could you print? (A figure can be repeated. For example, 313 is possible.)

How many different three-figure numbers could be printed?

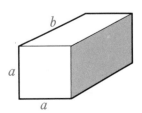

6.2 Highlands College sweatshirts are available in three sizes: small, medium and large. Buyers have a choice of five colours: red, blue, orange, yellow and green.

The college shop stocks all sizes and colours. How many different combinations of size and colour are there?

# 7 Inverse proportionality

7.1 If some gas is compressed into a smaller volume (without any gas escaping) its pressure increases. 'Boyle's law' says that the pressure is inversely proportional to the volume.

(a) If the volume is reduced to $\frac{1}{2}$ of what it was to start with, what happens to the pressure?

(b) If the volume is reduced to $\frac{1}{3}$ of what it was to start with, what happens to the pressure?

(c) Some gas occupies a volume of 5 litres and its pressure is 100 mb. If the gas is compressed to a volume of 2 litres, what will its pressure be?

7.2 A banjo string 38 cm long is tuned to the note B whose frequency is 496 Hz.

What length of the string will give the note D whose frequency is 588 Hz?

# 8 Using algebra

8.1 Write a formula, in terms of $a$ and $b$, for

(a) the volume of this prism

(b) the total surface area of the prism

8.2 Imagine a pattern of squares and triangles like this, with *n* squares.

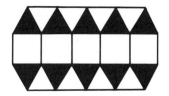

Write a formula for

(a) the number of black triangles

(b) the number of white triangles

(c) the total number of triangles

8.3 Re-arrange each of these formulas to make *p* the subject.

(a) $c = ap - k$      (b) $m = \dfrac{px}{y}$      (c) $f = h - sp$

# 9 Trigonometry (3)

9.1 Calculate the lengths marked with letters.

(a)               (b)               (c)

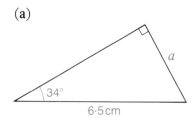
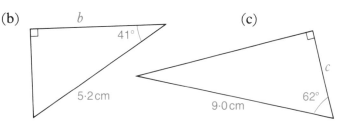

9.2 Calculate the lengths marked with letters.

(a)               (b)               (c)

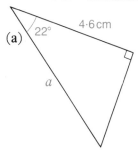
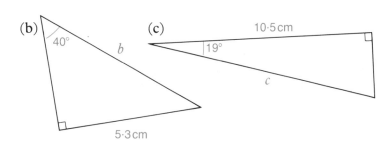

9.3 Two roof beams are each 5·5 m long, and the angle between them is 113°.

(a) What is the size of the angle marked θ?

(b) Calculate the distance AB, to the nearest metre.

85

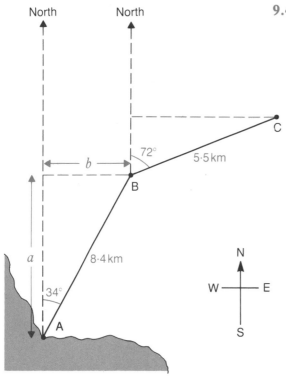

**9.4** The map on the left shows the path of a motor boat.

For the first part of its journey, AB, it travelled on a bearing of 034° (34° clockwise from north) and covered 8·4 km.

For the second part of its journey, BC, it travelled on a bearing of 072° and covered 5.5 km.

(a) Calculate how far north of A is the point B. (This is the distance marked *a*.)

(b) Calculate how far east of A is the point B. (This is the distance marked *b*.)

(c) Calculate how far north of B is the point C.

(d) Calculate how far north of A is the point C.

(e) Calculate how far east of A is the point C.

## 10   Graphs and charts

**10.1** Criticise the poster shown on the left.

**10.2** Criticise the chart shown below.

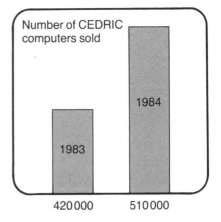

**10.3**  This graph shows how much protein is eaten per day, on average, in three different parts of the world.

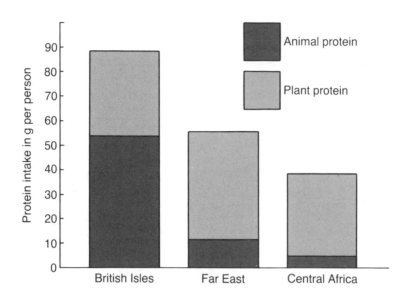

Estimate the percentage of animal protein in the daily protein intake in each of the three parts of the world.

# 11  Vectors

**11.1**  Write down each of these vectors as a column vector.

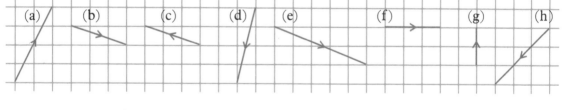

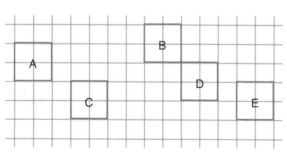

**11.2**  Write down the column vector of each of these translations.

(a) A to B    (b) B to A

(c) A to C    (d) B to D

(e) C to E    (f) E to B

# Money matters : Saving

Most people save up for their holidays or Christmas, or for something special.
But where do they keep their savings? Under the mattress, in tins, etc.?

Money left around the house is not very safe.
And as prices rise, the money will buy less and less.

The money could be put into a bank deposit account, or a Post Office Savings account, or a building society account, etc.

When you save money in this way, the bank or building society etc. pays you for leaving your money with them. The amount they pay you is called **interest**.

Why is the bank willing to do this? The reason is that the bank lends the money to other people, who pay the bank even more interest than the bank pays you. In that way the bank covers its costs and makes a profit.

Banks and building societies have various savings schemes, each with its **annual interest rate**.

Suppose the interest rate is 8% p.a. (p.a. = per annum, or per year).

In one year, your savings will grow by 8%.
So every £1 (or 100p) will become £1·08 (or 108p).

In other words, in one year your savings will be
**multiplied by 1·08**.

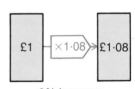
8% increase

1·08 is the **multiplier** for an 8% increase.

This is what will happen if you invest £500 to start with, at 8% p.a.

**Start**        **After 1 year**        **After 2 years**        **After 3 years**

£500 ─── ×1·08 ──→   £540 ─── ×1·08 ──→   £583·20 ─── ×1·08 ──→   £629·86 ──[

1. Anar invests £80 in a bank deposit account.
   The interest rate is 6% p.a.

   (a) What is the multiplier for a 6% increase?

   (b) Calculate the amount in Anar's account, to the nearest penny,
   after   (i) 1 year    (ii) 2 years    (iii) 3 years

2. Jonathan invests £60 in a building society.
   The interest rate is 10% p.a.

   (a) What is the multiplier for a 10% increase?

   (b) Calculate the amount in Jonathan's account after 4 years.

3. Susan invests £150 in a building society, at 8·5% p.a.

   (a) What is the multiplier for an 8·5% increase?

   (b) Calculate the amount in Susan's account after 3 years.

Suppose £500 is deposited in a savings account, and the
interest rate is 10% p.a.

Each year the amount is multiplied by 1·1. This diagram shows
how the amount grows. (The amounts are rounded off to the nearest £.)

But if prices are rising too at the same rate, then although the
amount grows, it will not be worth any more than it was
to start with.

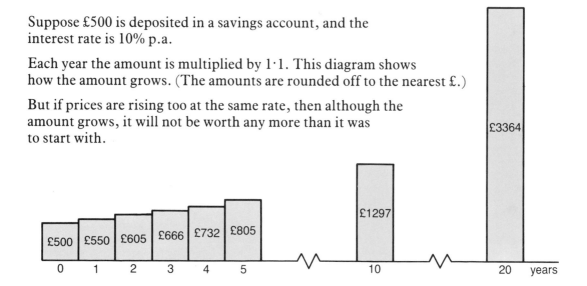

For example, suppose you want to buy a motorbike which costs £800.
You invest £500 with the idea that after 5 years you will have £805,
and so will be able to afford the bike. If prices are rising at 10% p.a.
as well, after 5 years the same bike will cost nearly £1300!

89

## Regular savings

Some savings schemes offer a higher interest rate if you agree to pay in a certain amount regularly, for example every month.

Suppose you pay in £20 on the 1st day of each month, starting on 1st July. Suppose the monthly interest rate is 1%.

In each month the amount in the account is multiplied by 1·01.

This is what happens.

| Date | Amount in account |
|---|---|
| 1st July | £20 |
| 31st July | £20·20 |
| 1st Aug | £40·20 |
| 31st Aug | £40·60 |
| 1st Sept | £60·60 |
| 30th Sept | £61·21 |

You start by paying in £20 on 1st July.

By 31st July the amount is multiplied by 1·01.
£20 × 1·01 = £20·20

On 1st August you pay in £20, so the total amount at the start of August is £40·20.

By 31st August the amount is multiplied by 1·01.
£40·20 × 1·01 = £40·60, to the nearest p.

On 1st September you pay in £20, so the total amount at the start of September is £60·60.

By 30th September the amount is multiplied by 1·01,
£60·60 × 1·01 = £61·21.

And so on.

4 Continue the calculation above until you get to 31st December.

5 Tim gets a job and decides to save £50 a month out of his wages. He opens a savings account which offers him a monthly interest rate of 1·2%. He starts by paying in £50 on 1st May.

(a) What is the multiplier for a 1·2% increase?

(b) Make a table similar to the one above, up as far as 31st August.

---

[1] A **monthly** rate of 1% is equivalent to a **yearly** rate of 12·68%, because if £1 is left in for a year it gets multiplied by 1·01 every month, in other words twelve times, and

$$£1 \times 1·01 \times 1·01 \times 1·01 \times 1·01 \times 1·01 \times 1·01 \times 1·01 \times 1·01 \times 1·01 \times 1·01 \times 1·01 \times 1·01 = \textbf{£1·1268}.$$

# 12 Mappings

## A Reflection

The triangle ABC has been reflected in the dotted line, to give the triangle A′ B′ C′.

The triangle ABC in its starting position is called the **object** of the reflection. The result of reflecting the object is called the **image**.

We also use the words **object** and **image** when talking about individual points.
For example, A is an object and A′ its image.

(When a letter is used to name a point, then the image is usually shown by using the same letter with a dash.)

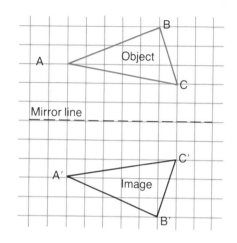

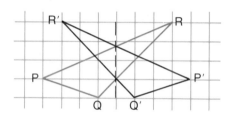

In mathematics we always think of mirrors as being double-sided.

Points on one side are reflected on to the other, and vice versa.

It is easy to reflect a point in a mirror which is on a grid line, by counting squares.

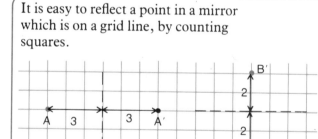

When the mirror line is at 45° to the grid lines, we can count squares diagonally.

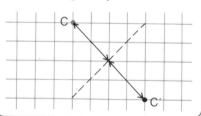

**A1** Copy each diagram and reflect the shape in the dotted line.

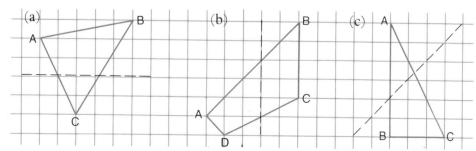

## B 180° rotation

*You need worksheet R3–1, tracing paper.*

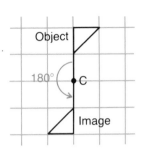

In this diagram the upright flag has been rotated through 180° about the point C.

The flag in its starting position is called the **object** of the rotation. The new position is called the **image**.

The point C is called the **centre of rotation**.

The centre of rotation does not have to be a point on the object itself.

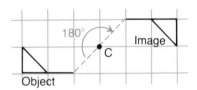

The example below shows how tracing paper can be used to find the position of an image after a 180° rotation.

This object is to be rotated through 180° about C.

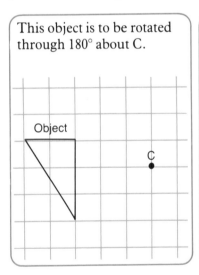

Trace the object and the centre of rotation. Then rotate the tracing through 180° (half a complete turn) keeping the point C fixed.

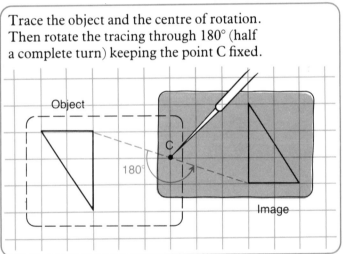

*The diagrams for questions B1 to B4 are on worksheet R3–1.*

**B1** In each case draw the image of the object after a 180° rotation about C. Use tracing paper if you wish.

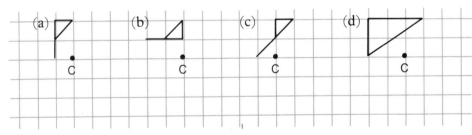

**B2** Each diagram below shows an object together with its image after a 180° rotation. Mark the centre of rotation in each case.

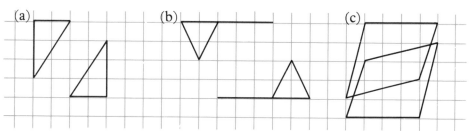

**B3** Draw the image of each object after a 180° rotation about C. Do it without using tracing paper.

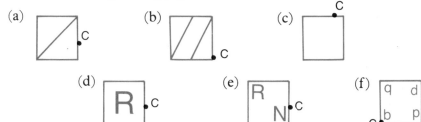

Here is a simple way to find the image of a point after a 180° rotation.

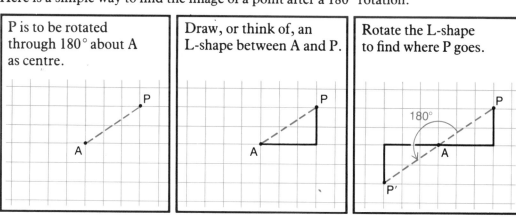

| P is to be rotated through 180° about A as centre. | Draw, or think of, an L-shape between A and P. | Rotate the L-shape to find where P goes. |

**B4** Use the L-shape method to find the image of each point P, Q and R after a 180° rotation about A. Then join up P', Q', R' to make the image of triangle PQR.

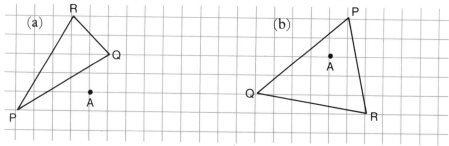

93

## C 90° rotation

You need worksheet R3–2, tracing paper.

This diagram shows how tracing paper can be used to find the image of an object after a 90° rotation about a centre.

In this case the rotation is **anticlockwise**.

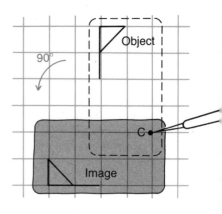

*The diagrams for questions C1 to C5 are on worksheet R3–2.*

**C1** In each case draw the image of the object after a rotation of 90° anticlockwise about C. Use tracing paper if you wish.

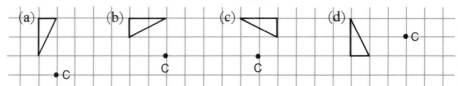

**C2** *Without using tracing paper*, draw the image of each object after a rotation of 90° anticlockwise about C. Afterwards check your answers with tracing paper.

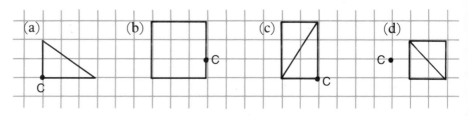

The L-shape method can also be used for a 90° rotation.

| P is to be rotated through 90° anticlockwise about A. | Think of, or draw, the L-shape, as before. | Rotate the L-shape to find where P goes to. |
|---|---|---|
| 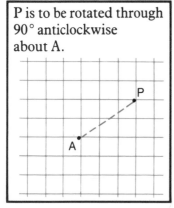 | 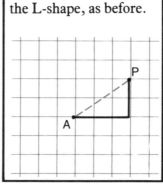 | 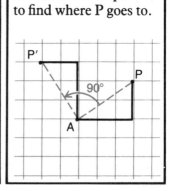 |

**C3** (a) Find the image of P after a 90° anticlockwise rotation about A. Label it P′.

(b) Rotate P′ through 90° anticlockwise about A, and mark the image P″.

(c) Rotate P″ in the same way to get P‴.

(d) Join up PP′P″P‴. What shape is it and where is A in relation to it?

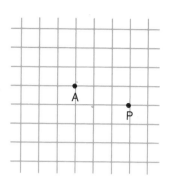

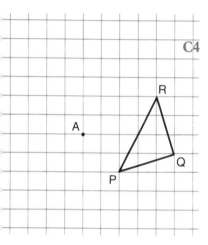

**C4** (a) Use the L-shape method to rotate each point P, Q, R though 90° anticlockwise about A. Join up P′Q′R′.

(b) Rotate P′Q′R′ in the same way to get P″Q″R″.

(c) Rotate P″Q″R″ in the same way to get P‴Q‴R‴.

(d) What kind of symmetry does the pattern of four triangles have?

**C5** Each diagram shows an object and its image after a 90° rotation. The rotation may be clockwise or anticlockwise. In each case the image is shaded.

See if you can find the centre of each rotation. Use tracing paper to check when you think you may have found the centre.

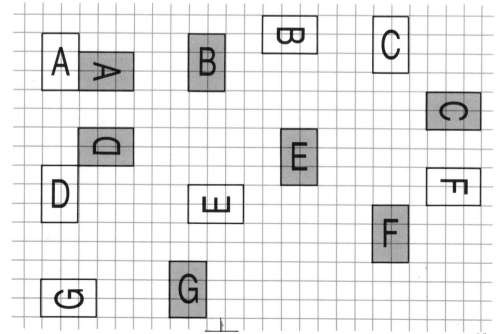

# D Translation

In a translation, every point moves the same distance and in the same direction.

A translation can be described by a column vector. The diagram on the right shows a translation whose vector is $\begin{bmatrix} 4 \\ -2 \end{bmatrix}$.

Once again the new position of a point is called its image.

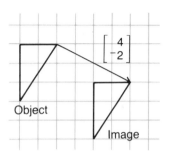

**D1** What is the column vector of each of these translations? The **image** is shaded in each case.

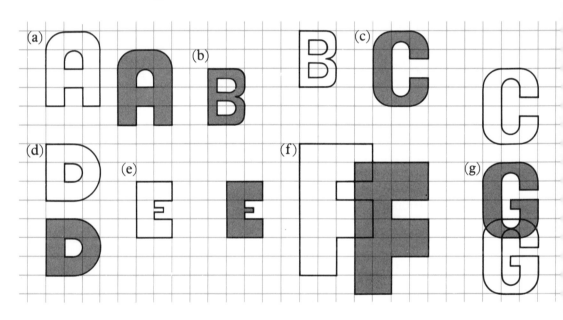

# E Congruence

**Congruent** means 'having the same shape and the same size'.

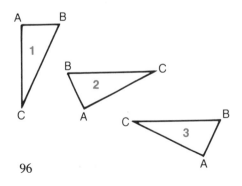

**E1** Triangles 1, 2 and 3 are congruent. Trace triangle 1.

(a) Can you fit your tracing over triangle 2 without turning the tracing paper over? What about triangle 3?

(b) The lettering of triangle 1 goes clockwise round the triangle. Which way does it go on triangle 2? Which way on triangle 3?

We say that triangle 1 (at the bottom of the previous page) is
**directly congruent** to triangle 2, but **oppositely congruent** to triangle 3.

E2 This question is easy to do if you use tracing paper.
Do it without tracing paper.

For each shape below say whether it is
directly congruent or oppositely congruent
to the shape shown on the right.

*a* *b* *c* *d*

*e* *f* *g* *h*

## F  Mappings

A reflection can thought of as a 'machine'.
The inputs are objects and the outputs are images.

When a reflection is thought of in this way, it
is called a **mapping**, and we say each object
is **mapped onto** its image.

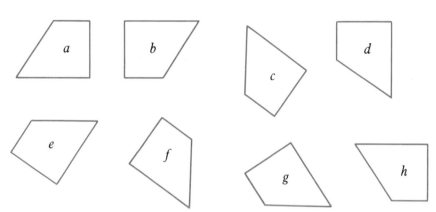

A reflection produces an image which is oppositely congruent to the
object. The **sense** of the lettering is changed (from clockwise to anticlockwise, or vice versa).

Rotations and translations are also mappings. They produce an image
which is directly congruent to the object.

In the diagrams below, ↻ and ↺ show the sense of the lettering.

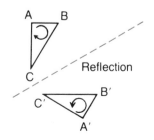

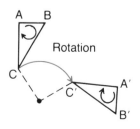

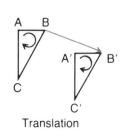

In some questions below you are asked to describe a mapping.
You first say whether it is a reflection, a rotation or a translation.
If it is a reflection, you give the mirror line (e.g. its equation).
If it is a rotation, you give the centre, angle and sense (clockwise or anticlockwise).
If it is a translation, you give the column vector.

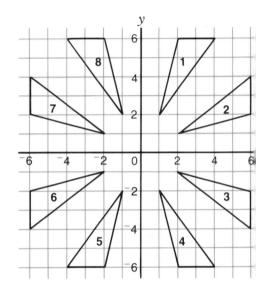

**F1** (a) Which triangles are directly
   congruent to triangle 1?

  (b) Which triangles are oppositely
    congruent to triangle 1?

  (c) Describe the mapping which
    maps triangle 1 onto

      (i) triangle 3

      (ii) triangle 5

      (iii) triangle 6

      (iv) triangle 8

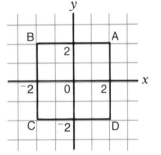

**F2** The square ABCD shown on the left is the object.
  Each diagram below shows the image of ABCD after a mapping.
  Describe the mapping in each case.

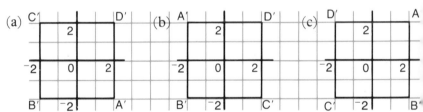

*The diagrams for questions F3 to F9 are on worksheet R3–3.*

**F3** ABCD is the square cross-section of a heavy box standing on the floor.
  The box is rolled along the floor. First it is rotated about A as
  shown, until B is on the floor. Then it is rotated about the new
  position of B, and so on until it is the same way up as before.

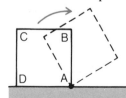

Draw and letter each position of
the box, and draw the path traced
out by the point D as the box rolls.

98

**F4** This is a **plan** showing a heavy cupboard PQRS standing against a wall. The cupboard is moved as follows:

(1) It is first rotated 90° anticlockwise about R;
(2) then it is rotated 90° clockwise about the new position of S;
(3) then it is rotated 90° clockwise about the new position of R;
(4) finally it is rotated 90° anticlockwise about the new position of S.

Draw and letter each intermediate position of the cupboard, and the final position.

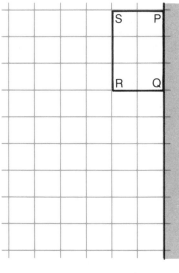

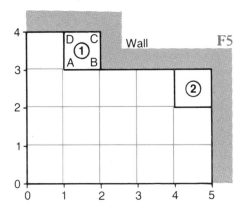

**F5** A safe, labelled ABCD in this plan, is to be moved from position 1 to position 2. It is very heavy and it is only possible to move it by rotating about any one corner.

Show how the safe can be moved from position 1 to position 2. Draw and label each intermediate position. Label the final position.

Describe each mapping.

**F6**

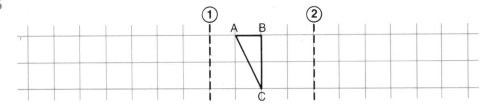

(a) Reflect triangle ABC in line 1. Label the image A′B′C′.

(b) Reflect triangle A′B′C′ in line 2. Label the image A″B″C″.

(c) Describe the single mapping which maps ABC onto A″B″C″.

**F7** Use a new copy of the diagram given in question F6.

(a) Reflect triangle ABC first in line 2. Label the image A′B′C′.

(b) Reflect A′B′C′ in line 1. Label the image A″B″C″.

(c) Describe the single mapping which maps ABC onto A″B″C″.

When you stand between two parallel mirrors which face each other you can see a sequence of images, alternately facing you and facing away from you.

We shall now see why this happens.

There are in fact two sequences of images.
To get the first sequence we start by reflecting the person in mirror 1, to get image 1.
Image 1 is then reflected in mirror 2 to get image 1,2.
Image 1,2 is reflected in mirror 1 to get image 1,2,1; and so on.

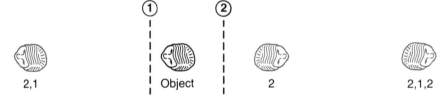

For the second sequence we start by reflecting the person in mirror 2, to get image 2.
Image 2 is reflected in mirror 1 to get image 2,1.
Image 2,1 is reflected in mirror 2 to get image 2,1,2; and so on.

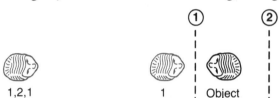

When the two sequences are put together, we get this.

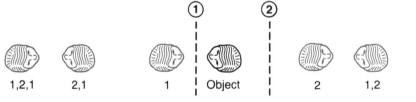

If the mirrors are moved so that they are no longer parallel, this is the effect on the images.

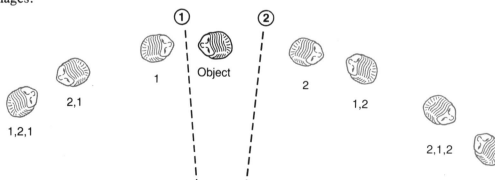

By adjusting the angle between the mirrors, we can make the images form a closed 'ring'.

In this example the angle between the mirrors is 30°.

A 'kaleidoscope' works in this way. The angle between the mirrors is usually 60°.

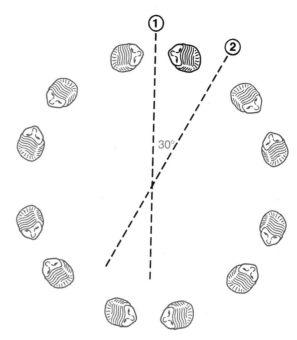

F8 In the diagram on the left, the angle between the mirrors is 60°.

Images 1 and 1,2 are already drawn.

Complete the diagram by drawing and labelling these images:

1,2,1     2     2,1

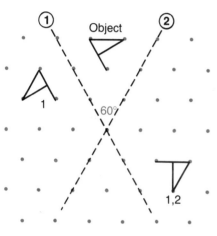

*F9 (a) Draw and label the complete set of images for this diagram.

The angle between the mirrors is 72°.

(b) Now get two mirrors and place them in position along the lines so that they meet at the centre of the circle.

How many images do you see?

Why can you not see all of the images you have drawn?

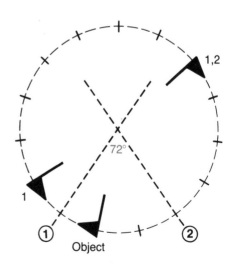

# 13 Trigonometry (4)

## A Calculating angles

You can calculate an angle in a right-angled triangle
when you know the lengths of two of the sides.

**Worked example**

Calculate the angle θ in this triangle.

Here we know 'hyp' and 'adj', so the formula to use is
$$hyp \times \cos \theta = adj.$$

So $10 \cdot 6 \times \cos \theta = 4 \cdot 8$.

So $\cos \theta = \dfrac{4 \cdot 8}{10 \cdot 6} = 0 \cdot 45283 \ldots$

We now need to find the angle whose cosine is $0 \cdot 45283 \ldots$
It is the **inverse cosine** of $0 \cdot 45283 \ldots$
On most calculators you find it by entering $0 \cdot 45283 \ldots$ and pressing $\boxed{inv}$ $\boxed{cos}$ .
The result (to the nearest degree) is 63°.

> **A1** Calculate, to the nearest degree, the angles marked with
> letters in these triangles.

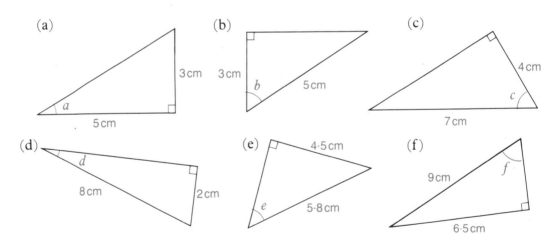

> **A2** A plank 5·3 metres long leans against the side wall of
> a house. The foot of the plank is 2·1 metres from the wall.
>
> Draw a sketch and calculate the angle which the plank
> makes with the ground, to the nearest degree.

**A3** A tree 2·50 metres tall casts a shadow 4·36 metres long.

Calculate the angle of elevation of the sun to the nearest degree. (The angle is marked *a* in the diagram.)

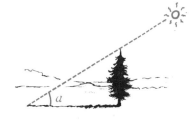

**A4** This is a diagram of some roof beams.

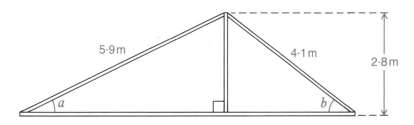

Calculate the angles marked *a* and *b*.

**A5** Calculate the side or angle marked with a letter in each of these right-angled triangles. Give lengths to the nearest mm and angles to the nearest degree.

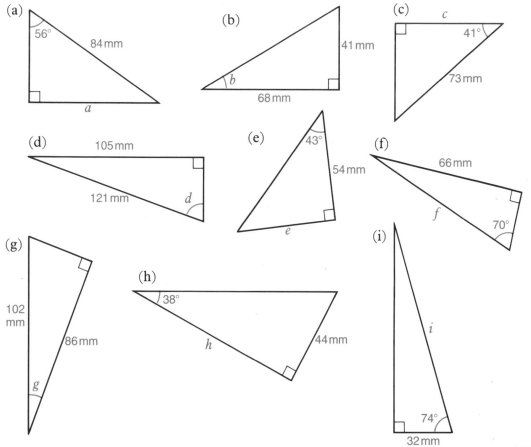

## B Mixed problems

The first step in answering each of these questions is to find
a suitable right-angled triangle in the diagram. You then
sketch the triangle, mark on it the measurements you know,
and use a letter for the side or angle you want to find.

Mark the sides of the triangle 'hyp', 'opp' and 'adj', and use
one of the basic formulas to calculate the unknown side or
angle.

In the first few questions the right-angled triangle has been
picked out for you in red.

B1 Calculate the angle which the line AB
makes with the horizontal, to the
nearest degree.

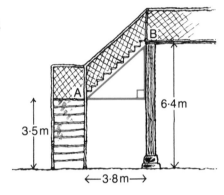

B2 (a) Calculate the height of the points P and Q
above the water level, to the nearest 0·1 metre.
(b) Calculate the distance between P and Q.

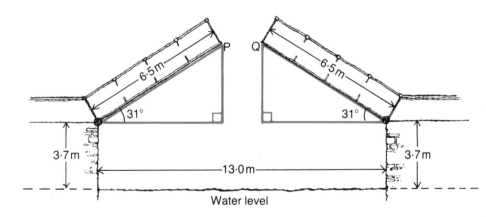

Water level

B3 Do question B2 again, but this time with each part
of the bridge making an angle of 48° with the horizontal.

B4 If the points P and Q in the diagram for question B2
are each 9·5 metres above the water level, what angle
does each part of the bridge make with the horizontal?

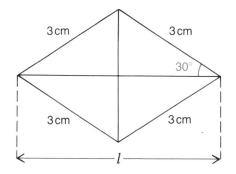

3 cm  3 cm

30°

3 cm  3 cm

*l*

**B5** Calculate the length marked *l* in this diagram.

## Isosceles triangles

An **isosceles** triangle is one with two equal sides.

An isosceles triangle can be split into two identical right-angled triangles. This fact is often useful in calculations.

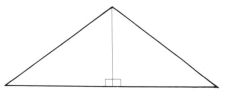

**B6** ABC is an isosceles triangle.
The angle ABC is 46°.

AB and BC are both 10 cm.

(a) What is the size of the angle marked θ?

(b) Calculate the length marked *a*, to the nearest 0·1 cm.

(c) Write down the length of AC.

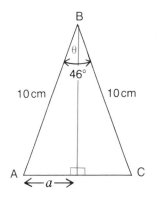

B

θ

46°

10 cm   10 cm

A         C

←*a*→

**B7** Do question B6 again, but with AB and BC each 12 cm long, and the angle ABC 112°

**B8** Each angle of a regular pentagon is 108°.

If a regular pentagon has sides which are each 8 cm long, calculate the length of one of its diagonals, to the nearest 0·1 cm.

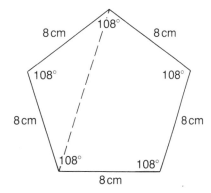

8 cm  108°  8 cm

108°        108°

8 cm            8 cm

108°    108°

8 cm

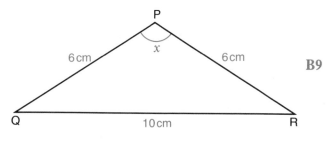

P

*x*

6 cm    6 cm

Q         R

10 cm

**B9** Calculate the angle marked *x* in the diagram on the left.
(Split the triangle PQR into two right-angled triangles first.)

105

## C  Pythagoras' rule

Pythagoras' rule connects the three sides of a right-angled triangle.

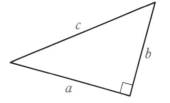

If the two shorter sides are of length $a$ and $b$ and the hypotenuse is of length $c$, then

$c^2 = a^2 + b^2$.

If you know the lengths of two of the sides of a right-angled triangle, Pythagoras' rule can be used to calculate the third side.

### Worked example

Calculate AB in this right-angled triangle.

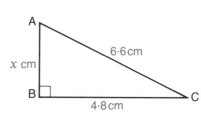

Let the length of AB be $x$ cm.

Pythagoras' rule tells us that $\quad x^2 + 4{\cdot}8^2 \quad = 6{\cdot}6^2$

$$\text{So} \quad x^2 + 23{\cdot}04 = 43{\cdot}56$$

$$\text{So} \qquad\qquad x^2 = 43{\cdot}56 - 23{\cdot}04 = 20{\cdot}52$$

$$\text{So} \qquad\qquad x = \sqrt{20{\cdot}52} = 4{\cdot}5 \text{ (to 1 d.p.)}$$

The length of AB is $4{\cdot}5$ cm (to 1 d.p.).

**C1**  Calculate, to the nearest $0{\cdot}1$ cm, the third side of each of these right-angled triangles.

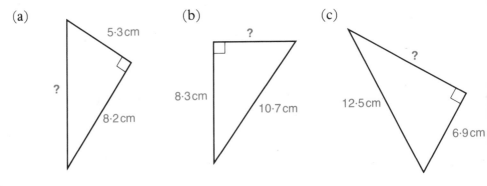

(a)   5·3 cm   ?   8·2 cm

(b)   ?   8·3 cm   10·7 cm

(c)   ?   12·5 cm   6·9 cm

**C2**  In this triangle, calculate

(a)  the length of PR

(b)  the angle of RPQ (marked $\theta$)

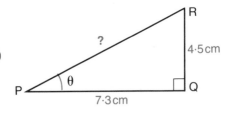

**C3** This diagram shows the end view of a house.

Calculate

(a) BC

(b) AB

(c) the angle BAC (marked θ)

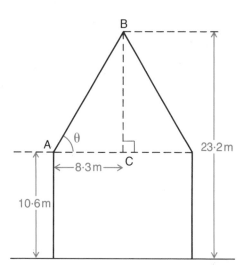

**C4** The diagram below shows a support made from steel bars.

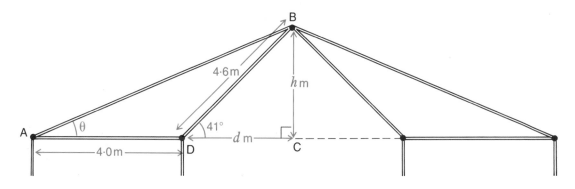

Calculate

(a) the height BC, marked *h*

(b) the distance DC, marked *d*

(c) the distance AC

(d) the length of the bar AB

(e) the angle which AB makes with the horizontal, marked θ

**C5** This diagram shows the front end of a tent.

Calculate

(a) the length of the sloping edge, marked *s*

(b) the angle at which this edge slopes to the horizontal

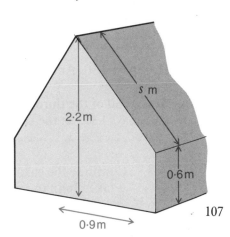

# Money matters : Borrowing

Suppose you want to buy something expensive. You may decide to borrow the money from a bank. The bank will charge you interest on the amount you borrow. The higher the rate of interest, the costlier is the loan.

A simple kind of loan is one which is made for a fixed period, and where the borrower repays the full amount (including interest) at the end of the period.

For example, suppose Anar borrows £500 for 4 years, and the interest rate is 20% p.a.
In each year, the amount she owes is multiplied by 1·2.

> After 1 year she owes £500 × 1·2 = £600.
>
> After 2 years she owes £600 × 1·2 = £720.
>
> After 3 years she owes £720 × 1·2 = £864.
>
> After 4 years she owes £864 × 1·2 = £1036·80.
>
> Then she repays £1036·80 and cancels the debt.

A more common way to repay a loan is by **instalments**.

Suppose John borrows £100. The interest rate is 15% p.a.
He agrees to pay back £30 at the end of each year until the debt is cancelled.

In each year, the amount John owes is multiplied by 1·15.

> After 1 year, John owes £100 × 1·15 = £115.
>
> He repays £30. At the start of the next year he owes £115 − £30 = £85.

> He starts the second year owing £85. During the year this amount is multiplied by 1·15.
>
> So at the end of the second year, John owes £85 × 1·15 = £97·75.
>
> He repays £30. At the start of the third year he owes £97·75 − £30 = £67·75.

> At the end of the third year he owes £67·75 × 1·15 = £77·91 (to the nearest p).
> He repays £30. At the start of the next year he owes £77·91 − £30 = £47·91.

1    Continue the calculation above and find out how many years it takes John to repay the debt.

In the previous question you were given the interest rate and the size of the instalments, and were asked to find out how long it would take to repay the loan.

In practice, the calculation is usually done a different way round.

First the bank decides on the interest rate.
Then the bank and the borrower between them decide how long the loan will be for, that is, how long it will take the borrower to repay it.

Then they decide whether the instalments are to be paid yearly, or every six months, or monthly, etc.

Then the bank calculates what size the instalments have to be so that the loan is repaid fully by the end of the agreed period.

Most personal loans are repaid in monthly instalments.
When people buy things on **hire purchase**, they are being given a loan by a hire purchase company. The repayments are usually monthly.

The interest rate for a loan is usually called the **annual percentage rate** (APR).
The table below shows the size of monthly instalments when £100 is borrowed at various different APRs.

### Time to full repayment

|  |  | 1 year | 2 years | 3 years | 4 years | 5 years |
|---|---|---|---|---|---|---|
|  | 20% | £9·19 | £5·01 | £3·63 | £2·96 | £2·56 |
|  | 22% | £9·27 | £5·09 | £3·72 | £3·05 | £2·65 |
| APR | 24% | £9·35 | £5·17 | £3·80 | £3·13 | £2·75 |
|  | 26% | £9·42 | £5·25 | £3·89 | £3·22 | £2·84 |
|  | 28% | £9·50 | £5·33 | £3·97 | £3·31 | £2·93 |
|  | 30% | £9·58 | £5·41 | £4·06 | £3·40 | £3·03 |

To find the monthly instalments for loans of amounts other than £100, you scale up or down.
For example, the instalments for a loan of £150 are 1·5 times those for a loan of £100.

2  Use the table to find the size of the monthly repayments on a loan of £250 at APR 26% repaid over 3 years.

3  What are the monthly repayments for a loan of £80 at APR 22% repaid over 5 years?

When a bank or hire purchase company offers a loan they tell you the APR.

The higher the APR, the more expensive is the loan.

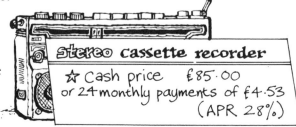

# 14 Points, lines and planes

## A Planes

Sometimes a drawing shows an 'object'
made up of lines and flat surfaces.
But the lines and surfaces are arranged
in an impossible way.

You can only tell that they are impossible
if you know what arrangements really
are possible.

This is what this chapter is about.

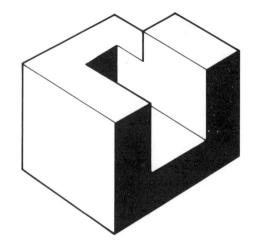

In this picture of a cube . . .     . . . you can see parts of 3 **planes**.

A plane is flat, and it is important to realise that it does not stop
at the bit you can actually see. It extends as far as you like in
all directions.

What you can see may have a gap
in it, but the plane does not.

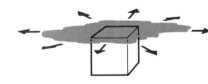

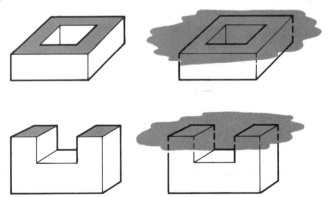

**A1** Here are two models. The surfaces which are visible are lettered. In model (a), the surfaces $d$ and $e$ are parts of the same plane.

For each model, say which surfaces go together as parts of the same plane.

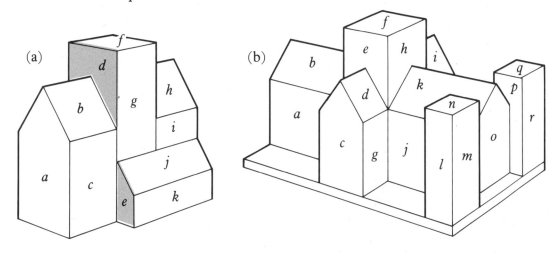

(a)

(b)

This picture seems to show a plane passing behind itself, which is impossible.

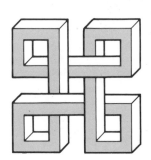

**A2** Which of these pictures show impossible objects?

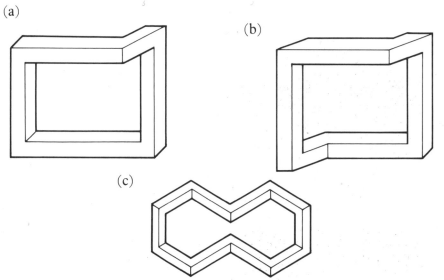

(a)

(b)

(c)

## B Two planes

*You need worksheet R3–4.*

When two planes meet, they make a straight **line** where they meet.

Each plane extends as far as you like.
The line where they meet stretches as far as you like in both directions.

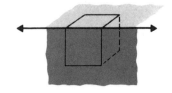

In your classroom, the walls are probably parts of planes.
So are the ceiling and the floor. Look for the lines where two planes meet.

Sometimes the parts of planes which we can see do not meet, but when we extend them we find the lines still exist.

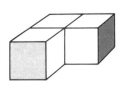

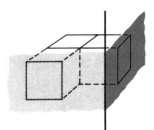

**B1** The surface AFIH is part of one plane. The surface CDEG is part of another plane.

The line where the two planes meet is one of the lines in the picture. Which line is it?

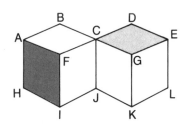

**B2** Do two planes always meet?

**B3** These diagrams are reproduced on worksheet R3–4. In each case draw on the worksheet the line where the two shaded planes meet.

(a)

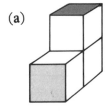

(b)

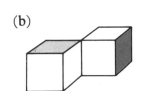

(c)

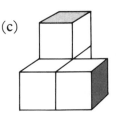

## Parallel planes

Two planes do not always meet.
They may be **parallel** to each other.
In that case they never meet, but are
the same distance apart everywhere.

In your classroom the floor and ceiling are
probably parallel to each other.

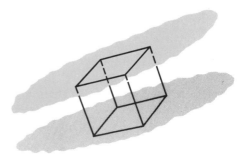

## An impossible object

 At first glance, it looks as though this object might be possible.
But what we know about two planes meeting in a line shows
that the object is not possible.

The two planes $a$ (front) and $b$ (top)
should meet in **one** line.

But according to the picture they meet
in two different lines! This is impossible.

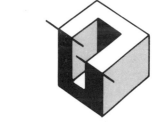

C4   Which of these pictures show impossible objects?

(a)
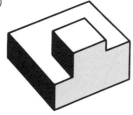

(b)
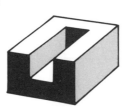

(c)

(d)

(e)

(f)
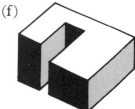

## C A plane and a line

If we have one plane and one line, three different things can happen.

The line may be **parallel** to the plane. The two never meet and they have no points in common.

The line may meet the plane in a **single point**.

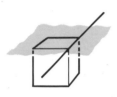

The line may lie entirely in the plane.
**All** the points on the line are then in the plane.

One of these three things must always happen.
There are no other possibilities.

**C1** Sketch this model house.
  (a) Show on your sketch where the line marked in red meets the shaded plane.
  (b) Mark on your sketch one line which is parallel to the shaded plane.

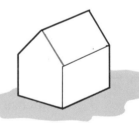

**C2** Does this picture show a possible object? If not, why not?

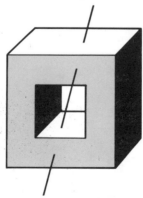

**C3** What about these?

(a)

(b)

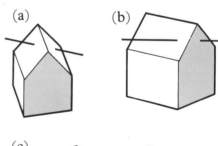

(c)

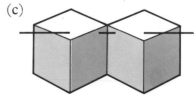

## D Three planes

Next we look at what can happen if we have three planes, *a*, *b* and *c*.

One possibility is that they are all parallel,
rather like the layers of a sandwich.

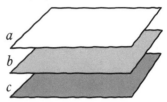

Otherwise two of the planes must meet, making a line.
Suppose *a* and *b* meet in a line. Then there are three things
which could happen.

| | | |
|---|---|---|
| The line may be parallel to the third plane *c*. So there is no point shared by all three planes. | The line may meet the third plane *c* in a point. So there is just one point shared by all three planes. | The line may lie entirely in the third plane *c*. So the three planes share a whole line of points. |

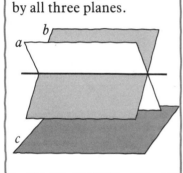 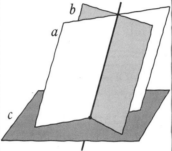 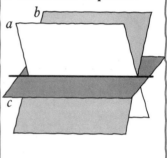

**D1** Find an example in your classroom of three planes which meet in a single point.

**D2** These diagrams are on worksheet R3–4. On the worksheet mark the point where the three shaded planes meet.

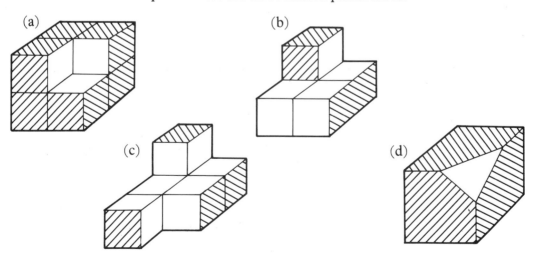

(a)

(b)

(c)

(d)

**An impossible object**

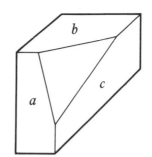

Planes $a$, $b$ and $c$ should meet at a point.

| Line 1 contains all the points shared by planes $a$ and $b$. | Line 2 contains all the points shared by planes $b$ and $c$. | Line 3 contains all the points shared by planes $c$ and $a$. |
|---|---|---|
| 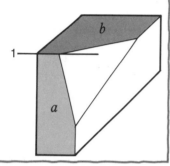 | 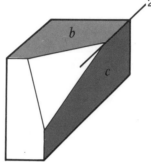 | 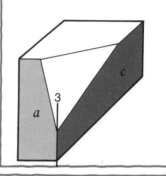 |

The point where planes $a$, $b$ and $c$ meet should be on all three of these lines.

So lines 1, 2 and 3 should all pass through one point.

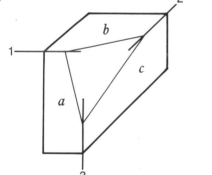

But they don't!
This means that the picture shows an impossible object.

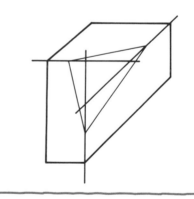

**D3** These drawings are on worksheet R3–4. Find out if they show impossible objects.

(a)

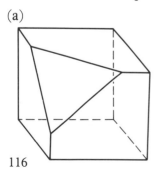

(b)

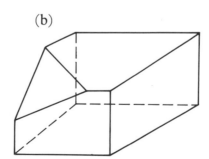

(c)

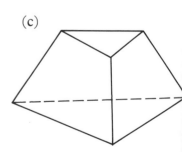

**D4** These diagrams are on worksheet R3–4. Find out if they show impossible objects.

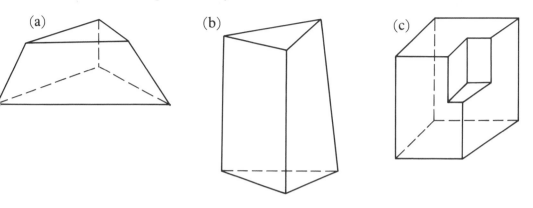

(a)         (b)         (c)

**D5** This is a collection of miscellaneous 'objects'. Which of these drawings show impossible objects?

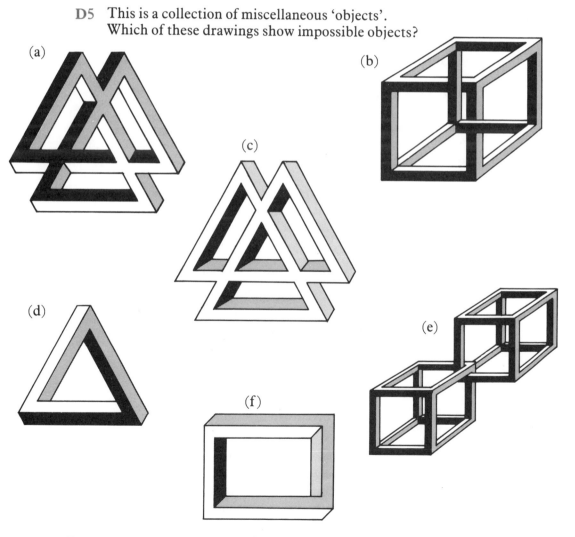

(a)    (b)    (c)    (d)    (e)    (f)

**D6** Try to draw an impossible object of your own.

117

# Money matters: Foreign exchange

When you travel abroad, you need to have foreign currency.

In France, you need French **francs**, in Italy you need **lire**, in Spain **pesetas**, etc.

You can 'buy' foreign currency from a bank or 'bureau de change'. The amount you get for every pound is called the exchange rate.

Exchange rates vary from day to day. Over long periods they may change quite considerably.

| BUREAU DE CHANGE | |
|---|---|
| FRANCE | 11·86 |
| ITALY | 2350 |
| SPAIN | 225 |
| GREECE | 151 |
| GERMANY | 3·89 |
| HOLLAND | 4·36 |
| AUSTRIA | 27·25 |
| USA | 1·45 |
| CANADA | 1·80 |

1 If the exchange rates are as shown in the picture above, how many French francs would you get for   (a) £50   (b) £80

2 How much would you have to pay (in £) for 500 francs?

3 In France, a restaurant advertises three set menus, costing 35F, 54F and 72F. Calculate the cost of each of these in pounds and pence.

**Travellers' cheques** are a good way to take money abroad. You can change them for money when you get there. Each cheque is for your own personal use only, and if you lose one you do not lose any money, provided you report the loss quickly.

Travellers' cheques can be issued in £ sterling, US dollars, French francs, etc.

When you change money, the bank or bureau de change charges you a small amount (called 'commission') for the transaction.

When you leave the foreign country, or when you get home, you may have some foreign money left. If you go to change it back into Sterling, you will find that the exchange rates for changing foreign money into Sterling are slightly different from the rates for changing Sterling into foreign money. From your point of view the rates are slightly worse: you don't get back quite as much as you would expect.

# 15 Formulas and graphs

## A  Substituting numbers into formulas

First of all a reminder: $3a^2$ means $3 \times (a\text{-squared})$.

For example, if $a$ is 5, then $3a^2 = 3 \times (5^2) = 3 \times 25 = 75$.

> **A1** Calculate
>
> (a) $4x^2$ when $x$ is 3    (b) $5t^2$ when $t$ is 4    (c) $\frac{1}{2}s^2$ when $s$ is 2
>
> (d) $10y^2$ when $y$ is 5    (e) $0 \cdot 1b^2$ when $b$ is 6    (f) $2u^2$ when $u$ is $0 \cdot 5$

The next questions are to give you practice in using formulas.

> **A2** $s$ and $t$ are connected by the formula $s = t^2 + 2t + 5$.
> You can calculate $s$ for different values of $t$ like this:

$$s = t^2 + 2t + 5$$

When $t = 0$,   $s = (0 \times 0) + (2 \times 0) + 5 = 0 + 0 + 5 = 5$
When $t = 1$,   $s = (1 \times 1) + (2 \times 1) + 5 = 1 + 2 + 5 = 8$
When $t = 2$,   $s = (2 \times 2) + (2 \times 2) + 5 = 4 + 4 + 5 = 13$

> Write the next three lines, for $t = 3$, $t = 4$ and $t = 5$.

> **A3** Copy this formula and complete the four lines of working.

$$b = 20 - 3a^2$$

When $a = 0$,   $b = 20 - 3 \times 0^2 = 20 - 0 = 20$
When $a = 1$,   $b = 20 - 3 \times 1^2 =$
When $a = 2$,
When $a = 3$,

> **A4** $p$ and $q$ are connected by the formula $q = 2p^2 - p$.
>
> Calculate $q$ when $p$ is    (a) 5    (b) 8    (c) 10

> **A5** $c$ and $d$ are connected by the formula $d = 2c^2 - 3c + 7$.
>
> Calculate $d$ when $c$ is    (a) 0    (b) 1    (c) 5    (d) 8

When $x$ is a negative number, then $x^2$ is **positive**.

For example, if $x$ is $^-3$, then $x^2 = {}^-3 \times {}^-3 = 9$.

**A6**  $x$ and $y$ are connected by the formula $y = x^2$.

(a) Copy and complete this table of values of $x$ and $y$.

| $x$ | $^-5$ | $^-4$ | $^-3$ | $^-2$ | $^-1$ | 0 | 1 | 2 | 3 | 4 | 5 |
|---|---|---|---|---|---|---|---|---|---|---|---|
| $y$ | | | | | | | | | | | |

(b) Draw axes on graph paper. Suitable scales are:
Across: 1 cm to 1 unit; up: 1 cm to 5 units.

Plot the points from the table. Draw a smooth curve through them. Label the graph '$y = x^2$'.

(c) From your graph find as accurately as you can the **two** values of $x$ for which $y = 20$.

(d) Use a calculator to check that when you square each of these values of $x$, you get approximately 20.

You have to be particularly careful when you use negative numbers in formulas.

**Worked examples**

(1) If $b = 3a^2 - 1$, what is $b$ when $a$ is $^-4$?

$b = 3a^2 - 1$

$\quad = 3 \times (^-4)^2 - 1$

$\quad = (3 \times 16) - 1$

$\quad = 48 - 1$

$\quad = 47$

(2) If $y = x^2 - 3x$, what is $y$ when $x$ is $^-2$?

$y = x^2 - 3x$

$\quad = (^-2)^2 - (3 \times {}^-2)$

$\quad = 4 - {}^-6$

$\quad = 4 + 6$

$\quad = 10$

(3) If $s = 4r - 2r^2$ what is $s$ when $r$ is $^-3$?

$s = 4r - 2r^2$

$\quad = (4 \times {}^-3) - (2 \times {}^-3^2)$

$\quad = {}^-12 - (2 \times 9)$

$\quad = {}^-12 - 18$

$\quad = {}^-30$

**A7**  If $y = x^2 - 5x$, what is $y$ when $x$ is

(a) 10  (b) 7  (c) 2  (d) 0  (e) $^-1$  (f) $^-3$  (g) $^-10$

**A8**  If $q = 2p - p^2$, what is $q$ when $p$ is

(a) 5  (b) 1  (c) 0  (d) $^-2$  (e) $^-4$  (f) $^-5$  (g) $^-10$

**A9**  If $t = 3s^2 - 4s$, what is $t$ when $s$ is

(a) $^-2$  (b) $^-8$  (c) 3  (d) 1  (e) 0  (f) $^-4$  (g) $^-1$

## B Graphs from formulas

When a stone is thrown vertically upwards, its height at any time afterwards can be calculated from a formula.

The formula is $h = ut - 5t^2$.

$h$ stands for the height of the stone, in m, above the point where it was thrown from.

$u$ stands for the speed, in m/s, with which the stone was thrown.

$t$ stands for the time in seconds since the stone was thrown.

**B1** Suppose a stone is thrown vertically upwards with a speed of 80 m/s. $u$ is 80, so the formula for $h$ becomes $h = 80t - 5t^2$.

Calculate the height of the stone 3 seconds after it was thrown.

**B2** A stone is thrown vertically upwards with a speed of 50 m/s.

(a) Write down the formula for $h$ when $u$ is 50.

(b) Calculate $h$ when $t$ is 4.

**B3** A stone is thrown vertically upwards with a speed of 40 m/s. The formula connecting $t$ and $h$ is $h = 40t - 5t^2$.

(a) Copy and complete this table of values of $t$ and $h$.

| $t$ | 0 | 1 | 2 | 3 | 4 | 5 | 6 | 7 | 8 |
|-----|---|---|---|---|---|---|---|---|---|
| $h$ |   |   |   |   |   |   |   |   |   |

(b) Draw axes on graph paper. Use the scales shown here.

Plot the points from your table. Draw a smooth curve through them.

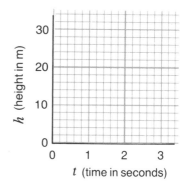

**Note.** The curve does **not** show the path of the stone through the air. The stone is thrown vertically upwards. The scale across represents **time**, not distance.

Use the graph to answer these questions.

(c) How high was the stone 1·5 seconds after being thrown?

(d) At what times was the height of the stone 30 metres?

(e) For how long was the stone's height greater than 65 metres?

121

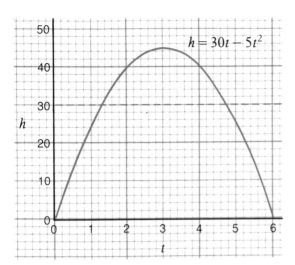

$$h = 30t - 5t^2$$

**B4** This is the graph you get when the stone is thrown at 30 m/s.

The formula in this case is

$$h = 30t - 5t^2.$$

(a) What is the maximum height the stone reaches?

(b) At what time is the stone's height 30 metres?

(c) Between what two times is its height greater than 20 metres?

**B5** A farmer has 20 metres of wire fencing.

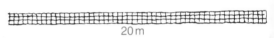

20 m

He uses it to make a rectangular sheep-pen against a stone wall. The wall forms one side of the pen.

Let $x$ metres be the length of each of the sides which are at right-angles to the wall.

They add up to $2x$ metres, leaving $20 - 2x$ metres for the other side.

$x$   $x$

$20 - 2x$

If $A$ is the area of the pen in m², then $A = x(20 - 2x)$.

Area $= x(20 - 2x)$

(a) Calculate the value of $A$ when $x$ is 0, 1, 2, 3, . . . and so on. Set out the working like this.

> $A = x(20 - 2x)$
>
> When $x = 0$, $A = 0 \times (20 - 0) = 0 \times 20 = 0$
>
> When $x = 1$, $A = 1 \times (20 - 2) = 1 \times 18 = 18$
>
> When $x = 2$, $A = 2 \times (20 - 4) = 2 \times 16 = 32$
>
> Carry on until $A$ is 0 again.

(b) Summarise the results of your calculations in a table of values.

| x | 0 | 1 | 2 | 3 | 4 | 5 | 6 | 7 | 8 | 9 | 10 |
|---|---|---|---|---|---|---|---|---|---|---|----|
| A |   |   |   |   |   |   |   |   |   |   |    |

(c) Draw axes on graph paper. Choose suitable scales yourself. Plot the points from your table and draw a graph of $(x, A)$.

(d) Use your graph to find the values of $x$ for which $A$ is 40.

B6 Another farmer has 16 m of fencing. She cuts it into two equal pieces.

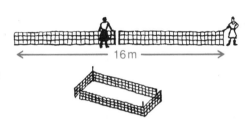

16 m

She bends each piece into an L-shape and fits them together to make a rectangular pen.

(a) Let $x$ m be the length of one side of the pen. Write down an expression for the length of the other side, in terms of $x$.

(b) If $A$ m$^2$ is the area of the pen, write a formula for $A$ in terms of $x$.

(c) Calculate $A$ when $x$ is 0, 1, 2, 3, . . . and make a table of values.

(d) Draw a graph of $(x, A)$.

(e) Use your graph to find the values of $x$ for which $A$ is 10.

This is the graph of $y = x^2 - 3x$, which we can also write $x^2 - 3x = y$.

We can use the graph to solve any equation of the form

$$x^2 - 3x = \text{a number.}$$

For example, to solve $x^2 - 3x = 5$, we look for the points of the graph where $y$ is 5.

The points are marked A and B. At A, $x$ is about $^-1\cdot2$, and at B about $4\cdot2$.

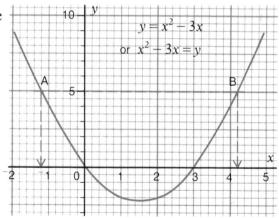

B7 From the graph above find (approximately) the two solutions of the equation (a) $x^2 - 3x = 2$ (b) $x^2 - 3x = {}^-1$

B8 Draw the graph of $y = x^2 - 2x$ for values of $x$ from $^-3$ to 5.
(a) Use it to solve the equations (i) $x^2 - 2x = 10$ (ii) $x^2 - 2x = 5$

(b) For what range of values of $x$ is $x^2 - 2x$ less than 3? Give your answer in the form 'Values of $x$ between . . . and . . .'.

123

# Review 3

## 12 Mappings

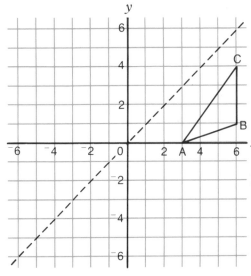

**12.1** Draw this diagram.

(a) Reflect the triangle ABC in the line $y = x$. Label the image A′B′C′.

(b) Reflect A′B′C′ in the y-axis. Label the new image A″B″C″.

(c) What single mapping will map triangle ABC onto triangle A″B″C″?

**12.2** Draw the diagram again.

This time reflect ABC first in the y-axis and then reflect the result in the line $y = x$.

What single mapping will map the triangle ABC onto the final image?

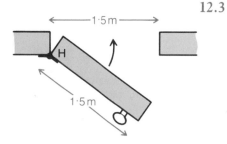

**12.3** This drawing is a plan of a door which is supposed to rotate about the hinge H and fit snugly into the gap between the two walls.
Will the door shut properly? If not, why not?

## 13 Trigonometry (4)

**13.1** Calculate the angles marked with letters, to the nearest degree.

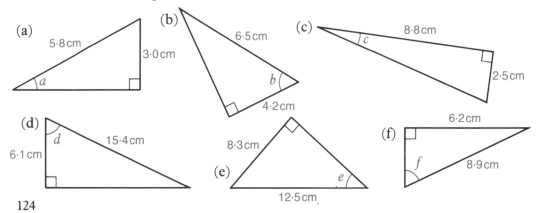

(a) 5·8cm  3·0cm  $a$

(b) 6·5cm  4·2cm  $b$

(c) 8·8cm  $c$  2·5cm

(d) $d$  6·1cm  15·4cm

(e) 8·3cm  12·5cm  $e$

(f) 6·2cm  $f$  8·9cm

**13.2** Calculate the sides and angles marked with letters.
Give lengths to the nearest 0·1 cm and angles to the nearest degree.

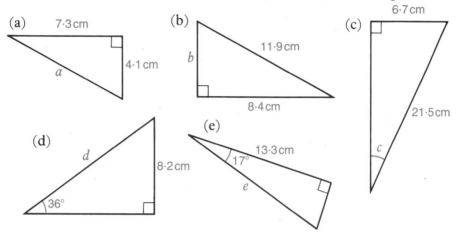

(a) 7·3 cm — 4·1 cm — $a$

(b) 11·9 cm — $b$ — 8·4 cm

(c) 6·7 cm — 21·5 cm — $c$

(d) $d$ — 8·2 cm — 36°

(e) 13·3 cm — 17° — $e$

# 14 Points, lines and planes

**14.1** ABCD is a piece of wire.
$p$ is a plane sheet of paper.

Which of the points A, B, C and D
are above the level of the plane $p$,
and which are below it?

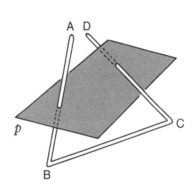

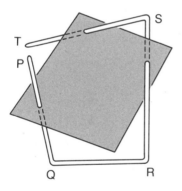

**14.2** Explain why this is a picture of
an impossible object.

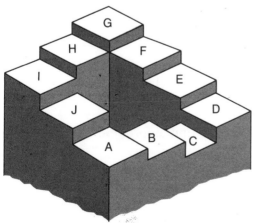

**14.3** This is not an impossible object.

(a) Draw a view of the object
looking down from above.
Letter the squares in your view.

(b) Which of the 'steps' in the
picture are not actually next
to one another?

125

# 15 Formulas and graphs

15.1   If $y = 4x - 5x^2$, calculate the value of $y$ when $x$ is

    (a) 3   (b) 10   (c) 1   (d) 0   (e) $^-2$   (f) $^-5$

15.2   If $q = 2p^2 - 3p + 1$, calculate the value of $q$ when $p$ is

    (a) 4   (b) 6   (c) $^-3$   (d) 0   (e) $^-4$   (f) $^-10$

15.3   $x$ and $y$ are connected by the formula $y = x^2 - 4x$.

    (a) Make a table of values of $x$ and $y$ for values of $x$ from $^-2$ to 6.

    (b) Draw a graph of $y = x^2 - 4x$.

    (c) Use your graph to find, approximately, the values of $x$ for which $x^2 - 4x = 6$.

    (d) For what range of values of $x$ is $x^2 - 4x$ less than 2? Give your answer in the form 'Values of $x$ between . . . and . . .'.

15.4   A woman has a rectangular pond 5 m by 6 m.

She wants to make a concrete path round the pond, the same width all round.

She has enough concrete to cover an area of 50 m². Her problem is: how wide can the path be?

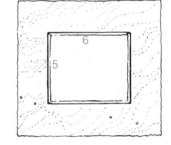

Suppose she makes a path whose width is $x$ metres.
The area of the path can be split up into squares and rectangles, as shown here.

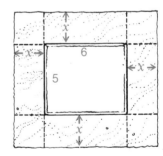

    (a) If $A$ m² is the area of the path, show that $A = 4x^2 + 22x$.

    (b) Calculate $A$ when $x$ is 0, 1, 2 and 3.

    (c) Draw a graph of $(x, A)$ and use it to find, approximately, the value of $x$ for which $A = 50$.

# 1 Whole numbers and decimals

1.1 Without using a calculator, say which of these you could buy with a £20 note.
(a) 38 metres of hosepipe at 47p per metre
(b) 4·5 metres of curtain fabric at £5·25 per metre
(c) 120 metres of nylon rope at 21p per metre

1.2 When Brenda puts her gas fire on 'high', the gas it uses costs 68p per hour. How much does it cost to have it on 'high'
(a) for 8 hours  (b) for $2\frac{1}{4}$ hours
(c) over the weekend, from 6 p.m. Friday to 8 a.m. Monday

1.3 Calculate these costs to the nearest thousand pounds.
(a) The cost of educating 225 children at £3260 each per year
(b) The cost of feeding 225 children at £970 each per year
(c) The cost of clothing 225 children at £125 each per year

1.4 (a) 6 people share a 5 kg sack of potatoes. What weight does each get?
(b) 5 people share a 6 kg sack. What weight does each get?

1.5 A station buffet sells coffee in standard cups (240 ml) at 38p, or in large beakers (330 ml) at 55p. Which is better value?

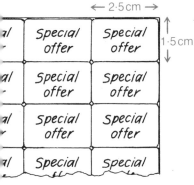

1.6 This picture shows a sheet of stick-on labels. Each label is 2·5 cm wide and 1·5 cm high. The sheet is 65 cm wide and 48 cm high.

How many labels are there on the sheet?

1.7 A bottle contains 0·6 litre of cough mixture. The 'adult dose' is three medicine spoonfuls. A medicine spoon holds 5 ml.

How many adult doses can you get from the bottle?

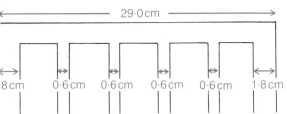

1.8 This diagram shows a page in a newspaper.
All five columns are the same width.

How wide is each column?

**1.9** Round off  (a) 37·886 to 2 d.p.    (b) 37·886 to 2 s.f.
                (c) 0·039 862 to 3 s.f    (d) 362 598 to 3 s.f.

**1.10** Write these numbers in standard index form.
       (a) 20 000 000   (b) 0·000 08   (c) 3 620 000   (d) 0·000 009 27

# 2 Percentage

**2.1** Re-write these statements using percentages.

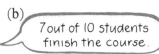

(a) I'll tell you what, I'll reduce the price by a quarter.

(b) 7 out of 10 students finish the course.

(c) $\frac{2}{5}$ of government expenditure goes on education.

**2.2** Calculate  (a) 45% of £280    (b) 8% of £17·50

**2.3** This table gives some information about 175 people living in a block of flats.

|  | Male | Female |
|---|---|---|
| Under 18 | 23 | 19 |
| 18 or over | 63 | 70 |

  (a) What percentage of the 175 people are males aged 18 or over?
  (b) What percentage are females under 18?
  (c) What percentage **of the males** are under 18?
  (d) What percentage of the under-18s are male?

**2.4** Gold jewellery is never made from 100% gold because it would be too soft. It is made from an alloy of gold and some other metal such as silver.

The amount of gold in the alloy is measured in 'carats'. The maximum number (for pure gold) is 24 carats. So '12 carat gold' is an alloy which has $\frac{12}{24}$ of its weight pure gold (in other words, $\frac{1}{2}$ or 50% of the alloy is pure gold.)

  (a) What percentage of '18 carat gold' is pure gold?
  (b) What percentage of '22 carat gold' is pure gold?
  (c) If you made an alloy which was 25% pure gold and 75% other metals, how could you describe it using carats?

**2.5** (a) Alice's salary is £8260. It goes up by 15%. What is it after the increase?
  (b) Ada's salary goes up from £7230 to £8240. What is the percentage increase?

**2.6** Calculate the percentage reduction in each of these, to the nearest 1%.

  (a) A car salesman reduces the price of a car from £3000 to £2750.
  (b) An estate agent reduces the price of a house from £49 500 to £47 500.
  (c) A dress shop reduces the price of a £75 dress by £20.

# 3 Fractions

**3.1** The sizes of five nuts (in inches) are $\frac{11''}{16}, \frac{1''}{2}, \frac{5''}{8}, \frac{15''}{16}$ and $\frac{3''}{4}$.
Put them in order of size, starting with the smallest.

**3.2** You are trying to tighten a bolt. A $\frac{3''}{4}$ spanner is just too small.
A $\frac{7''}{8}$ spanner is just too big. Which size is halfway between the two?

**3.3** 1 inch is equal to $25 \cdot 4$ mm.
What are these equal to in mm, to the nearest $0 \cdot 1$ mm?

(a) $\frac{1''}{4}$  (b) $\frac{3''}{4}$  (c) $\frac{5''}{8}$  (d) $\frac{13''}{16}$

# 4 Ratio

**4.1** The 'aspect ratio' of a cinema screen is the ratio $\dfrac{\text{width}}{\text{height}}$.

(a) Calculate the aspect ratio of each of these screens, to 2 d.p.

A: $5 \cdot 7$ m wide, $4 \cdot 3$ m high    B: $10 \cdot 6$ m wide, $5 \cdot 2$ m high
C: $7 \cdot 8$ m wide, $5 \cdot 2$ m high    D: $7 \cdot 2$ m wide, $4 \cdot 8$ m high

(b) Which of the four screens are similar to each other?

**4.2** Calculate these multipliers, to 3 significant figures.

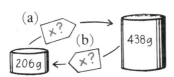

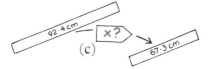

**4.3** In an equilateral triangle, the ratio $\dfrac{\text{height}}{\text{base}}$ is $0 \cdot 866$ (to 3 s.f.).

Use this fact to calculate
(a) the height of an equilateral triangle whose base is $4 \cdot 5$ cm
(b) the base of an equilateral triangle whose height is $7 \cdot 2$ cm

# 5 Gradient

**5.1** Calculate the gradient of
(a) AB    (b) BC    (c) AC

**5.2** These are rough sketches of two hills, P and Q.
Which hill is steeper, and why?

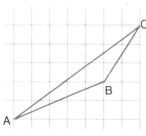

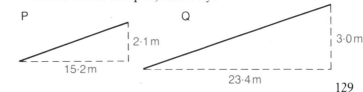

129

# 6 Rates

6.1 (a) A tap takes 12·5 minutes to fill a 60-litre water tank. Calculate the rate of flow of the tap in litre/min.

(b) How long would it take to fill the same tank from a tap which flows at 18·5 litre/min?

6.2 An oven is turned on. The temperature rises slowly at first, then faster, and then more slowly again until it reaches a maximum. Then it stays constant. Sketch a graph to show all this.

6.3 Worldwings Airways use AX7 aircraft on their flights from London to Moscow, a distance of 1880 miles. The flight takes $4\frac{1}{4}$ hours.

(a) Calculate the average speed of the aircraft.
(b) The airline considers replacing the AX7 by another plane, which can fly at an average speed of 530 m.p.h. If they do this, what will the new flight time be?

6.4 This table shows distances and times for a train journey.

| Distance from London (miles): | 0 | | 209 | 299 | | 401 |
|---|---|---|---|---|---|---|
| | London | | Preston | Carlisle | | Glasgow |
| Time: | 12:45 | | 15:30 | 16:45 | | 18:15 |

(a) Calculate the average speed of the train between
(i) London and Preston  (ii) Preston and Carlisle
(iii) Carlisle and Glasgow

(b) Calculate the overall average speed for the whole journey, to 1 d.p.

6.5 A solution of copper sulphate contains 0·85 g of copper sulphate per litre.
(a) How much copper sulphate is there in 0·35 litre of solution?
(b) What volume of the solution contains 0·50 g of copper sulphate?

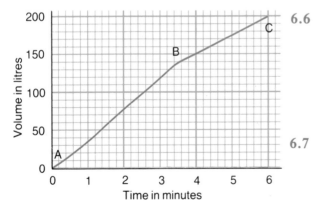

6.6 This graph shows the amount of liquid in a tank while it was being filled.

Calculate the average rate at which the water entered the tank
(a) between A and B
(b) between B and C

6.7 Pat is crossing the desert in a truck. She starts with a full fuel tank holding 140 litres of fuel. After travelling 80 miles she has used up 25 litres.

She still has 390 miles to go. Will she make it?

## 7 Negative numbers

7.1 Work out (a) $^-3 + 7$    (b) $^-2 + {}^-8$    (c) $6 + {}^-4$    (d) $^-5 + 3 + {}^-2$

7.2 Work out (a) $^-8 - 3$    (b) $^-4 - 9$    (c) $5 - {}^-1$   (d) $^-8 - {}^-2$
          (e) $^-6 - {}^-4$    (f) $^-2 - {}^-5$    (g) $3 + {}^-4 - {}^-1$

7.3 Work out (a) $^-4 \times 3$    (b) $^-5 \times {}^-2$    (c) $^-18 \div {}^-2$   (d) $20 \div {}^-4$

7.4 Work out the value of $p - qr$ when
     (a) $p = {}^-7, q = {}^-2$ and $r = 3$    (b) $p = 10, q = 4$ and $r = {}^-3$

7.5 Work out the value of $\dfrac{x + y}{x - y}$ when $x = {}^-7$ and $y = {}^-3$.

## 8 Constructing formulas

8.1 These arrangements are made with red and black balls joined together.

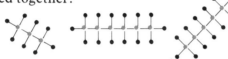

     (a) How many black balls will there be when there are 20 red balls?

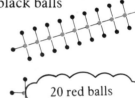
20 red balls

     (b) If there are $n$ red balls in the arrangement, write down an expression for the number of black balls.

$n$ red balls

8.2 A square like the one shown here is drawn on square spotty paper, except that it is $n$ by $n$ units instead of 3 by 3.
Write an expression for the number of spots
(a) on its boundary    (b) inside the square

## 9 Techniques of algebra

9.1 If $a = 5, b = 2$ and $c = {}^-3$, calculate
     (a) $a^2 + bc$    (b) $a - bc$    (c) $5b^2$    (d) $a(b - c)$    (e) $b^2 - 3c$
     (f) $\dfrac{b - c}{a}$    (g) $\left(\dfrac{a - c}{b}\right)^2$   (h) $ab - c^2$    (i) $\dfrac{a}{b} + c$    (j) $\dfrac{a}{b + c}$

9.2 If $V \text{m}^3$ is the volume of a sphere of diameter $d\,\text{m}$, then $V$ and $d$ are connected by the formula $V = \dfrac{\pi d^3}{6}$.

     Calculate $V$ to 2 s.f. when $d$ is   (a) $2 \cdot 5$    (b) $0 \cdot 38$

**9.3** Multiply out the brackets in each of these expressions.

    (a) $3(p+q)$    (b) $3(p+2q)$    (c) $5(a-3)$    (d) $a(b-a)$    (e) $xy(x+y)$

**9.4** Simplify each of these expressions, where possible.

    (a) $3n+5-2n+2$    (b) $5x-3y-2x-4y$    (c) $a+4-9-3a$
    (d) $2b-3c-5+a$    (e) $7u-8+1-5u$    (f) $10-2x-5+6x$

**9.5** Factorise each of these expressions.

    (a) $3a+6b$    (b) $4a-12$    (c) $ab^2+5b$    (d) $8ab-2a^2$

**9.6** A cylinder of radius $r$ cm and height $h$ cm is made of paper.

The cylinder can be cut and 'opened out' into three parts: two circles and a rectangle.

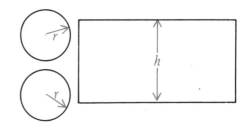

    (a) Write an expression for the length of the rectangle in terms of $r$.
    (b) Show that the total surface area of the cylinder is $2\pi r(r+h)$ cm$^2$.
    (c) Calculate the surface area when $r$ is 5·0 cm and $h$ is 10·0 cm.

# 10 Solving equations and re-arranging formulas

**10.1** Solve each of these equations.

    (a) $3x-17=28$    (b) $51=23+4x$    (c) $5x+25=5$
    (d) $8x+13=5x+4$    (e) $17-2x=8$    (f) $5=19-4x$

**10.2** Solve these equations. Give the value of $x$ to 2 d.p.

    (a) $2{\cdot}9x=11{\cdot}3$    (b) $0{\cdot}83x=0{\cdot}36$    (c) $\dfrac{x}{1{\cdot}6}=0{\cdot}28$    (d) $\dfrac{3{\cdot}5}{x}=0{\cdot}56$

**10.3** $P$, $V$, $R$ and $T$ are connected by the equation $PV=RT$.
    (a) Write a formula for $P$ in terms of the other letters.
    (b) Write a formula for $V$ in terms of the other letters.
    (c) Write a formula for $R$ in terms of the other letters.

**10.4** $u$, $v$ and $m$ are connected by the formula $m=\dfrac{u}{v}$.

    (a) Re-arrange the formula to make $u$ the subject.
    (b) Re-arrange the formula to make $v$ the subject.

**10.5** $a$, $b$, $c$ and $d$ are connected by the formula $d=ab-c$.
    (a) Calculate $b$, when $d=37$, $a=5$ and $c=3$.
    (b) Calculate $a$, when $d=17$, $b=4$ and $c=3$.
    (c) Re-arrange the formula so that $c$ is the subject.
    (d) Re-arrange the formula so that $a$ is the subject.

# 11 Algebraic graphs

**11.1** A worker in a trampoline factory is testing a spring. She hangs different weights on the spring and measures its length.
She finds that the length is related to the weight by the formula

$$l = 15 + \frac{w}{5}.$$

$l$ stands for the length of the spring in cm.
$w$ stands for the weight in kilograms hanging on it.

(a) Copy and complete this table.

| $w$ | 0 | 50 | 100 | 150 | 200 | 250 |
|-----|---|----|-----|-----|-----|-----|
| $l$ |   |    |     |     |     |     |

(b) Draw axes with the scales shown here. Draw the graph and label it with the formula.

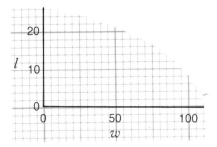

(c) Use the graph to find the length of the spring when 130 kg is hung from it.
(d) Use the graph to find what weight will make the spring 34 cm long.

**11.2** A boy leans out of a balcony and throws a ball upwards.
The height of the ball above the ground is given by the formula

$$h = 25 + 20t - 5t^2.$$

$h$ is the height above ground level, in m.
$t$ is the time in seconds since the ball was thrown.

(a) Calculate $h$ when $t$ is 0, 1, 2, 3, 4 and 5. Make a table of values.
(b) Draw a graph of $(t, h)$.
(c) Use the graph to answer these questions.
　(i) How high was the ball above the ground when it was thrown?
　(ii) What was the greatest height it reached?
　(iii) What happened 5 seconds after it was thrown?
　(iv) For how long was its height above the ground greater than 30 m?

**11.3** $x$ and $y$ are connected by the equation $y = x(5 - x)$.

(a) Make a table showing the value of $y$ when $x$ is 0, 1, 2, 2·5, 3, 4 and 5.

(b) Draw a graph of $(x, y)$

(c) From your graph find approximately the values of $x$ for which $x(5 - x) = 3$.

(d) Between which two numbers must $x$ lie if $x(5 - x)$ is greater than 5?

# 12 Proportionality

**12.1** A shop sells silver braid. The cost of the braid is proportional to the length bought. You can buy 40 cm for £1.00.

    (a) What will be the cost of (i) 120 cm  (ii) 60 cm  (iii) 30 cm  (iv) 90 cm
    (b) How much braid will you get for (i) £5  (ii) £2·50  (iii) £25

**12.2** Two towers stand side by side.
One tower is 32·5 m high and casts a shadow 45·1 m long.
The second tower's shadow is 58·3 m long.

    (a) Calculate the multiplier from the first shadow to the second shadow.

    (b) Calculate the height of the second tower, to the nearest 0·1 m.

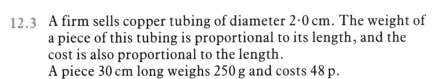

**12.3** A firm sells copper tubing of diameter 2·0 cm. The weight of a piece of this tubing is proportional to its length, and the cost is also proportional to the length.
A piece 30 cm long weighs 250 g and costs 48 p.

    (a) Calculate the weight and the cost of a 50 cm piece.
    (b) What length can you buy for £10?

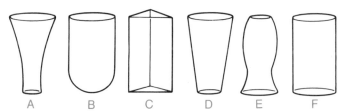

A    B    C    D    E    F

**12.4** In which of these containers will the volume of liquid be proportional to depth?

**12.5** A student studying electricity varied the voltage across a piece of wire and measured the current in the wire each time.
Here are her results. $V$ stands for the voltage, in volts, and $I$ for the current, in amps.

| $V$ | 1·5 | 2·2 | 3·2 | 4·3 | 5·0 |
|---|---|---|---|---|---|
| $I$ | 3·9 | 5·7 | 8·3 | 11·2 | 13·0 |

    (a) Draw axes with $V$ across and $I$ up. Plot the five points, and draw the graph of $(V, I)$.
    (b) Is $I$ proportional to $V$? How can you tell from the graph?
    (c) Find the gradient of the graph.
    (d) Write down the equation connecting $I$ and $V$ in the form $I = \ldots V$.

**12.6** Find the equation connecting $y$ and $x$ for each of these graphs.

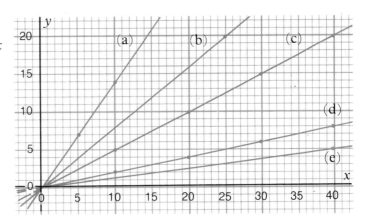

**12.7** The wavelength of a radio wave (measured in metres) is inversely proportional to the frequency of the wave (measured in kilohertz, kHz.)

BBC Radio 4 broadcasts on a frequency of 200 kHz with a wavelength of 1500 metres. BBC Radio 3 broadcasts on a frequency of 1215 kHz.

(a) Is the Radio 3 wavelength greater or less than the Radio 4 wavelength?

(b) Calculate the Radio 3 wavelength, to the nearest metre.

# 13 Loci

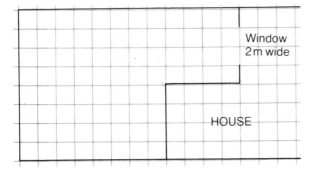

Window
2 m wide

HOUSE

**13.1** This is a plan of a back garden, drawn to a scale of $\frac{1}{2}$ cm to 1 m.

Copy the plan and colour the part of the garden which cannot be seen from the window.

**13.2** Two farmers living at A and B agree to dig a well and share it.

The well must be the same distance from A and from B, but it must be dug on land no higher than 10 m above sea-level.

(a) Trace or copy the map and show the possible positions of the well.

(b) Mark with a W the position which is closest to the farmhouses.

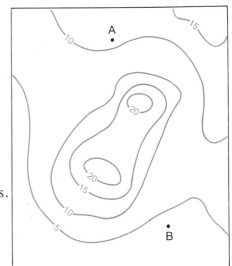

## 14 Area

**14.1** Each grid square on these two maps represents a square 20 km by 20 km.

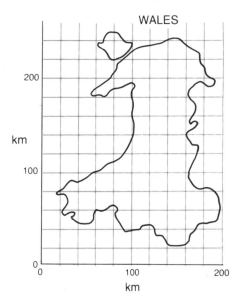

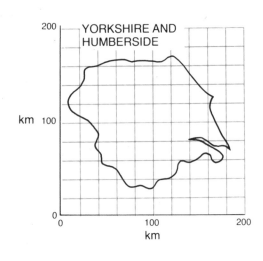

(a) What area does each grid square represent?

(b) Estimate the area of   (i) Wales   (ii) Yorkshire and Humberside
(Do not mark the maps. You can trace them if you like.)

(c) At the 1981 census, the population of Wales was 2 790 000,
and that of Yorkshire and Humberside 4 840 000.
Roughly how many people were there on average for each square
kilometre in   (i) Wales (ii) Yorkshire and Humberside

**14.2** Calculate the area of each of these shapes.

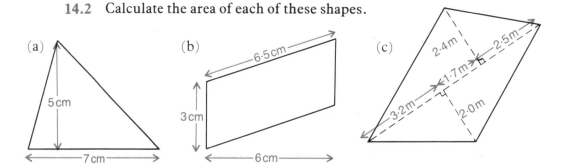

## 15 The circle

**15.1** Calculate the circumference of a circle of diameter 9·3 cm, to 2 s.f.

**15.2** Calculate the circumference of a circle of radius 5·8 cm, to 2 s.f.

**15.3**

You can buy a 'jacket' to fit round a hot water tank. It is made up of 'panels' like the one on the right.

20 cm wide

(a) About how many panels 20 cm wide would you need to go round a tank of diameter 42 cm? (Overestimate rather than underestimate.)

(b) About how many do you need to go round a tank 55 cm in diameter?

**15.4** This diagram shows a 'cloche'. It is made from transparent plastic and is used to protect growing plants.

Calculate the area of plastic used to make it.

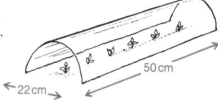

50 cm

←22 cm→

**15.5** Calculate the area of a circle of radius 8·3 cm, to 2 s.f.

# 16 Angles

**16.1** Calculate the angles marked with letters. (Two angles marked with the same letter are the same size.)

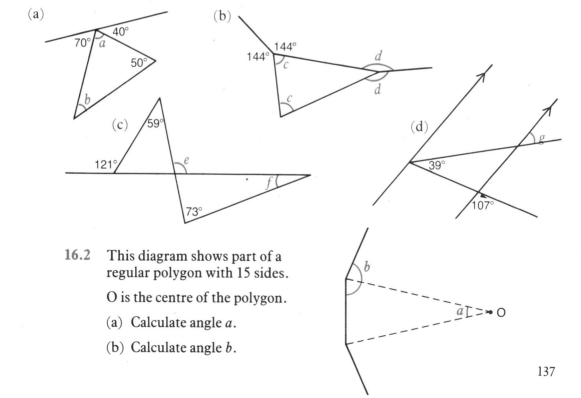

(a)

70° a 40°
50°
b

(b)

144° 144°
c d
d
c

(c) 59°

121° e
f
73°

(d)

39°
107°
g

**16.2** This diagram shows part of a regular polygon with 15 sides.

O is the centre of the polygon.

(a) Calculate angle a.

(b) Calculate angle b.

b

a ▷→ O

137

# 17 Scale drawing

17.1 The sketch on the right shows a greenhouse, and a cold frame standing next to it.

The sketch below shows the end of the greenhouse and cold frame. Measurements are in cm.

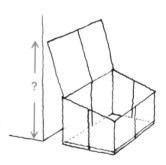

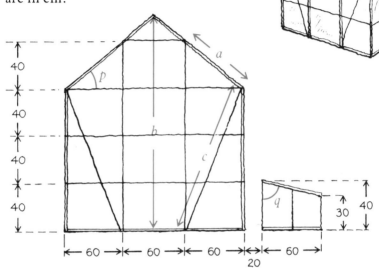

(a) Using a scale of 1 cm to 20 cm, make a scale drawing of the end of the greenhouse and cold frame.

(b) From the scale drawing, measure the lengths $a$, $b$ and $c$.

(c) Measure the angles $p$ and $q$.

(d) The lid of the cold frame is hinged. When it is open, it rests against the side wall of the greenhouse.

Use your scale drawing to find how far up the side of the greenhouse it touches.

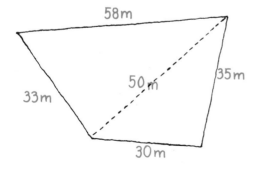

17.2 This is a rough sketch of a plot of land.

(a) Draw a plan to scale. Use a scale of 1 cm to 5 m. Describe how you made your drawing.

(b) Find out from your plan if it is possible to build a rectangular barn 40 m by 25 m on the plot. Describe how you found out.

# 18 Maps

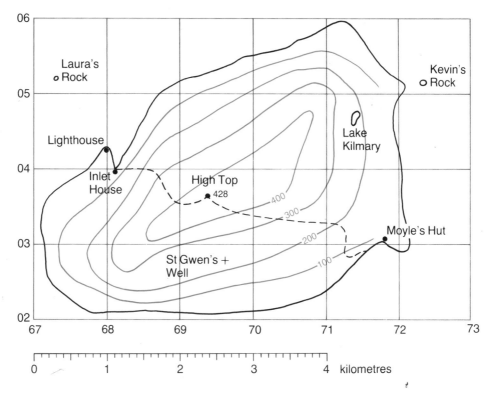

This is a map of an island.

18.1 (a) What is the four-figure grid reference of the square which Lake Kilmary is in?
(b) What is the six-figure grid reference of each of these?
(i) Inlet House    (ii) High Top      (iii) Moyle's Hut
(iv) Laura's Rock  (v) St Gwen's Well  (vi) Kevin's Rock

18.2 The height of St Gwen's Well above sea-level is between 200 m and 300 m. Find each of the points whose grid references are given below, and write the height at that point in the form 'between . . . and . . .'.

(a) 675032   (b) 683027   (c) 715036   (d) 695053   (e) 717040

18.3 There are two paths to High Top marked on the map. Which is steeper, the path from Inlet House or the path from Moyle's Hut? How can you tell?

18.4 Find the two points on the coast which are furthest apart and find the distance between them in km.

18.5 At low tide it is possible to walk all round the coastline of the island. Estimate the distance all round the island.

## 19 Symmetry

**19.1** If you reflect design A in the dotted line, which of those below will you see?

A

B                    C                    D

**19.2** Which of these 'words' have a 2-fold rotation centre?

(a) pod     (b) shoys     (c) bozzop     (d) onzuo

(e) dollop     (f) hoxoy     (g) poqdob     (h) snous

**19.3** Which of the four designs in question 19.1 have a 2–fold rotation centre?

**19.4** Draw this repeating strip pattern, and mark its lines of reflection symmetry and 2-fold rotation centres.

## 20 Vectors

**20.1** Write each of these vectors as column vectors.

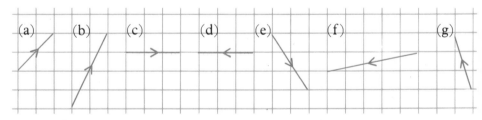

(a)   (b)   (c)       (d)   (e)       (f)           (g)

**20.2** Write down the column vector of the translation from
(a) A to B     (b) B to C     (c) C to D     (d) D to E
(e) E to F     (f) F to G

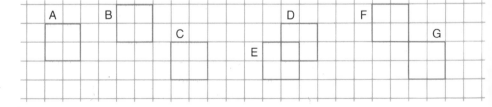

# 21 Mappings

**21.1** Copy each of these diagrams and draw the image of the shape after a 90° clockwise rotation about the point marked C.

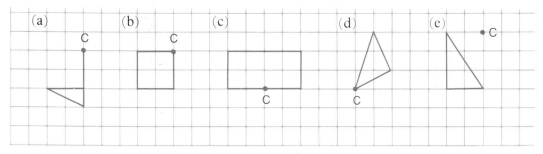

**21.2** Draw the diagram on the right.

(a) Reflect triangle XYZ in line *a*. Label the image X′Y′Z′.

(b) Reflect X′Y′Z′ in line *b*, and label the image X″Y″Z″.

(c) Which simple mapping maps XYZ onto X″Y″Z″?

(d) Do you get the same final image if you reverse the order of the reflections?

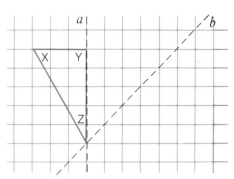

# 22 Three dimensions

**22.1** This is a plan of a house.

The pictures below are pictures of the house. From what direction (north, north-east, etc.) was each picture taken?

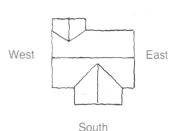

**22.2** A child's toy consists of a solid block of wood with four wheels. Here are a side elevation and a front elevation of the toy, drawn to a scale of 1 cm to 10 cm.

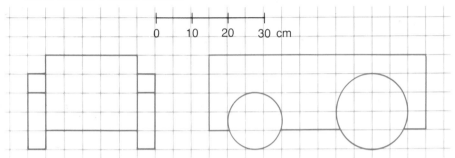

Draw, to the same scale, a plan view of the toy.

**22.3** This drawing shows the roof of a small shelter.

Imagine that the roof is cut along the edge AB, and flattened out to make a net.

(a) Draw the net to a scale of 1 cm to 1 m.

(b) Measure the net to find the area of the roof. Explain how you do it.

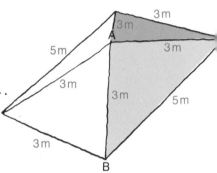

# 23 Volume

**Reminder.** 1 cm³ is equal to 1 millilitre (ml). 1 litre = 1000 ml = 1000 cm³.

**23.1** (a) Calculate the volume of this block, to the nearest 0·1 cm³.

(b) What would the block weigh if it was made of metal whose density is 8·5 grams per cm³? Give the weight to the nearest gram.

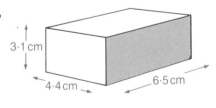

(c) What would the block weigh if it was made of plastic whose density is 0·85 grams per cm³?

**23.2** (a) Calculate the cross-sectional area of this prism.

(b) Calculate the volume of the prism.

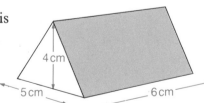

**23.3** This water tank can be filled to depth of 65 cm without overflowing.

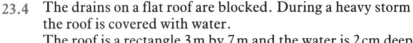

(a) Calculate the maximum volume of water in the tank
    (i) in cm³    (ii) in litres

(b) How deep is the water when the tank contains 250 litres?

**23.4** The drains on a flat roof are blocked. During a heavy storm the roof is covered with water.
The roof is a rectangle 3 m by 7 m and the water is 2 cm deep all over.

(a) Calculate the volume of the water, in cm³.
(b) What is that in litres?
(c) 1 litre of water weighs 1 kg. How much extra weight is the roof having to support because of the water?

**23.5** Here is a plan of a garden.

How many cubic metres of earth would be required to raise the soil level all over by 20 cm?

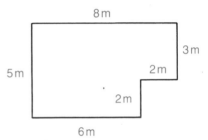

## 24 Enlargement and reduction

**24.1** What is the scale factor of each of these enlargements or reductions?

(a) A to B    (b) B to A    (c) C to A
(d) A to D    (e) D to C    (f) C to D

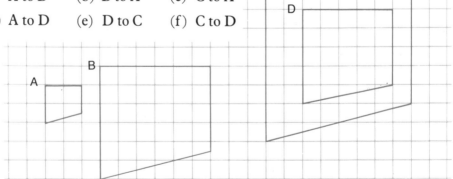

**24.2** (a) The picture shown here is to be enlarged so that its new width is 1155 mm.
Calculate its new height.

(b) If the picture is reduced to a height of 416 mm, calculate the new width.

143

## 25 Pythagoras' rule

**25.1** Calculate the side marked with a letter in each of these right-angled triangles. (All measurements are in cm.)

(a)

$a$

$4 \cdot 0$

$8 \cdot 0$

(b)

$b$

$4 \cdot 0$

$7 \cdot 0$

(c)

$5 \cdot 1$

$c$

$6 \cdot 8$

(d)

$7 \cdot 3$

$2 \cdot 9$

$d$

**25.2** The dotted lines on this map show the journey of a ship from A to B to C to D.

Calculate the length of each part of the journey and the total length of the journey.

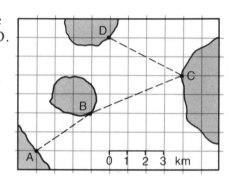

**25.3** The diagram below shows a type of car jack.

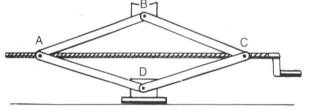

When the handle is turned, the points A and C move closer together, and the point B rises.

The lengths AB, BC, CD and DA are each 15 cm. Calculate the height of B above D when AC is 22 cm.

## 26 Trigonometry

**26.1** Calculate the lengths marked with letters. (All measurements in cm.)

(a)

$a$

$32°$

$7 \cdot 6$

(b)

$12 \cdot 4$

$74°$

$b$

(c)

$6 \cdot 5$

$c$

$52°$

(d)

$35°$

$d$

$6 \cdot 8$

**26.2** Calculate the angles marked with letters.

(a)

$a$

$24 \cdot 7$

$14 \cdot 3$

(b)

$b$

$6 \cdot 2$

$3 \cdot 6$

(c)

$2 \cdot 8$

$c$

$8 \cdot 3$

(d)

$7 \cdot 1$

$d$

$5 \cdot 3$

**26.3** A straight roadway is 10·4 m wide.
If you walk across it at an angle of
35° to an edge, how far do you walk?

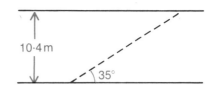

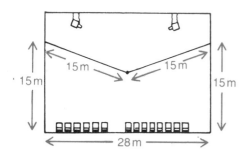

**26.4** The diagram on the left shows an end wall
of a house. The shape is symmetrical.

Calculate the angle which each of the sloping
lines makes with the horizontal.

**26.5** The diagram on the right shows the
symmetrical cross-section of a railway
embankment.

Calculate the angle which each
sloping side makes with the horizontal.

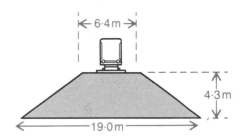

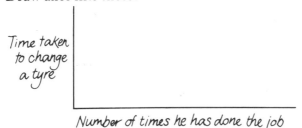

**26.6** A microphone is hung from the sides of
a school hall, as shown in this drawing.

Calculate the angle which each of the
two wires makes with the horizontal.

## 27 Interpreting graphs

**27.1** Karl is learning how to change the tyre on a wheel of a car.
As he does the job more and more often, he gets faster at it.
But eventually he gets to a point where he cannot do it any faster.

Sketch a graph showing how the time he takes to change a tyre
is related to the number of times he has done the job.
Draw axes like these.

Time taken
to change
a tyre

Number of times he has done the job

27.2 This sketch graph shows the amount of petrol in a car's tank during a journey.

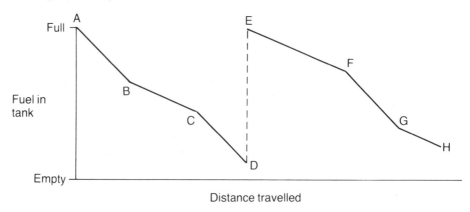

Distance travelled

The journey involved two kinds of driving: in towns and on main roads. In towns the car does fewer miles to a gallon than on main roads.

(a) Which parts of the graph show driving in towns? Explain how you decide.

(b) What does the dotted line DE show?

## 28 Statistics

28.1 Here are the weights in kilograms of the girls and the boys in a fourth-year class.

**Girls** 47, 61, 50, 50, 60, 55, 52, 54, 52, 50, 48, 53, 57, 54, 61
**Boys** 43, 59, 47, 59, 65, 62, 62, 58, 53, 70, 55, 57

(a) Draw two scales and mark the weights on them by dots.

(b) Calculate the mean weight of each group and mark its position on the scale.

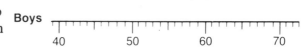

(c) In which group are the weights more widely spread out? Calculate the range for each group.

28.2 A firm sells paper clips in boxes marked 'about 100'. To check the contents, a sample of 20 boxes were opened and the clips counted.

| Number of clips in box | 95 | 96 | 97 | 98 | 99 | 100 | 101 | 102 |
|---|---|---|---|---|---|---|---|---|
| Number of boxes | | 1 | 2 | 4 | 4 | 7 | 1 | 0 | 1 |

Calculate the mean number of paper clips per box in the sample.

146

**28.3** Two wine 'experts' were asked to rate the quality of 15 different types of wine and to give each wine a score out of 10. Here are their scores.

| Wine | A | B | C | D | E | F | G | H | I | J | K | L | M | N | O |
|---|---|---|---|---|---|---|---|---|---|---|---|---|---|---|---|
| **1st expert** | 6 | 4 | 6 | 3 | 8 | 1 | 8 | 8 | 9 | 4 | 2 | 5 | 4 | 3 | 7 |
| **2nd expert** | 8 | 3 | 6 | 4 | 9 | 2 | 1 | 8 | 8 | 4 | 3 | 5 | 5 | 3 | 6 |

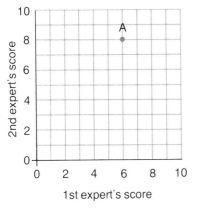

(a) Draw axes as shown on the left. Mark each pair of scores as a point on the diagram.

(b) Look at the diagram. Is there any particular wine which the experts disagree about very strongly? If so, which wine is it?

(c) Apart from this wine, is there a reasonable amount of agreement between the experts?

(d) Where would the points lie if the experts agreed on the score for every one of the wines?

(e) Calculate the mean of the scores given by the first expert. Do the same for the second expert. Which expert gave higher scores on average?

(f) The magazine which asked the experts to rate the wines wants to print an 'order of merit', showing the 15 wines in order of quality, best first. Suggest how they might make an 'order of merit'.

**28.4** Eight people work in the accounts department of a company.
The manager of the department is paid £260 a week.
The assistant manager gets £220 a week.
The manager's secretary gets £120 a week, and the assistant manager's secretary gets £100.

There are four clerical staff, each of whom gets £90 a week.

One of the clerical staff complains to her trade union that people in the accounts department are poorly paid. The manager tells the union that the average (mean) weekly pay in the department is £132·50.

(a) Show that the manager is right in what he says, by doing the calculation yourself.

(b) Why is the mean weekly pay misleading in this case?

# 29 Arranging and selecting

**29.1** A salesman starts from town S and goes on a tour, visiting each of the other towns once. One possible order for visiting them is CADB. How many different possible orders are there?

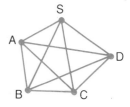

**29.2**  Stevie's Jeans are made in these waist measurements

26  28  30  32  34  36  38

and in these inside leg measurements

27  29  31  33

The factory makes jeans with every different possible combination of measurements, e.g. waist 38, inside leg 27.
How many possible combinations are there?

**29.3**  Four classes, A, B, C and D, each have practical exams in four subjects: science, woodwork, metalwork and home economics.

The exams all take place in a period of five days, from Monday to Friday.

Each exam lasts a whole day, and has to be done in the proper room. There is only one science room, one woodwork room, one metalwork room and one home economics room. In each room there is only enough space for one class at a time.

No class can have exams on four days running.

The home economics room is not available on Tuesday.

(a) Copy this exam timetable and complete it. Class A's exams are already fixed.

|   | Mon. | Tues. | Wed. | Thur. | Fri. |
|---|------|-------|------|-------|------|
| A | Sci. |       | H.E. | Wood. | Met. |
| B |      |       |      |       |      |
| C |      |       |      |       |      |
| D |      |       |      |       |      |

(b) Suppose it is Monday, not Tuesday, when the home economics room is not available. See if you can complete the timetable in this case. (All the other rules still apply.)

# 30  Probability

**30.1**  Jason has ten cards, numbered 2, 2, 3, 3, 3, 4, 5, 6, 8, 10.
He shuffles the pack and Anar picks one card at random.
What is the probability that Anar picks

(a) an even number    (b) a number less than 5    (c) a prime number

**30.2**  Audrey has five cards, numbered 1, 2, 3, 4, 5. She shuffles them and Kevin picks two cards at random.

(a) Make a list of all the possible pairs of cards Kevin could pick.

(b) What is the probability that Kevin picks a pair of consecutive numbers (e.g. 1 and 2 or 3 and 4, etc.)?

# M Miscellaneous questions

The questions in this section are taken from the SMP 11–16 pilot 16+ examination
(papers 2 and 3) and are reprinted with the kind permission of the Oxford and
Cambridge Schools Examination Board and the East Anglian Examinations
Board.

**M1** (a) One way to buy 3 litres of wine
is to buy three 1-litre bottles.
How much would this cost?

(b) Write down another way to buy
3 litres. How much would this cost?

(c) Write down yet another way to buy
3 litres. How much would this cost?

(d) Which is the cheapest way to buy
3 litres?

**M2** Carol has £12·50 to spend on records.
There are four records she would like to buy.

| A | B | C | D |
|---|---|---|---|

£4·30      £3·70      £4·60      £3·80

(a) She cannot afford to buy all four records.
How much **more** money would she need, to buy all four?

(b) She can afford to buy three of the records. (Remember she has £12·50.)
Which three could they be? (There are two answers. Give them both.)

**M3** The longest known species of seaweed is the Pacific giant kelp.
It can grow up to 60 metres in length, and can grow 45 centimetres
in a day.

If it is 20 m long now, and grows 45 cm every day, how many days
will it take from now to grow to its full length of 60 m?

Give your answer to the nearest whole number.

**M4** These drawings show two tiles of
the same thickness and made from
the same material.

The smaller tile weighs 24 g.

How much does the larger tile weigh?

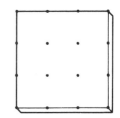

149

M5 The energy value of foods can be measured in calories.
This table gives the number of calories in 100 grams of various foods.

| Food | Number of calories in 100 g |
|------|------------------------------|
| White bread | 250 |
| Butter | 750 |
| Cheese | 400 |

A sandwich is made up of 50 g of white bread, 10 g of butter and 60 g of cheese.

(a) Calculate the number of calories in
    (i) the bread    (ii) the butter    (iii) the cheese

(b) Calculate the total number of calories in the sandwich.

M6 Here are two pictures of the sea, taken from above.
Picture B was taken **1 minute later** than picture A.
The dotted line shows the position of one particular wave.

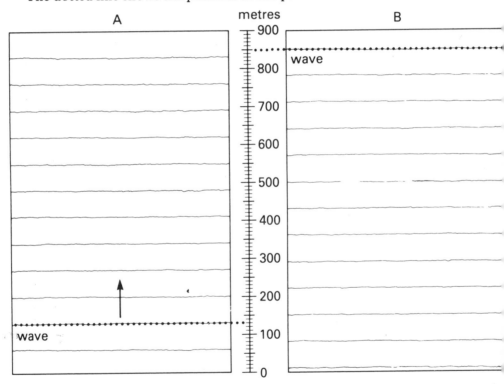

(a) How far did the dotted wave move in 1 minute?

(b) Calculate the speed of the wave, in metres per second.

(c) When the sea is fairly shallow, there is a formula for calculating
its depth when you know the speed of the wave. The formula is $d = \dfrac{s^2}{9 \cdot 8}$

    $d$ stands for the depth in metres.
    $s$ stands for the speed of the waves in metres per second.

    Use this formula to calculate the depth of the sea shown in the pictures.

M7 (a) Measure the angles marked $x$ and $y$.

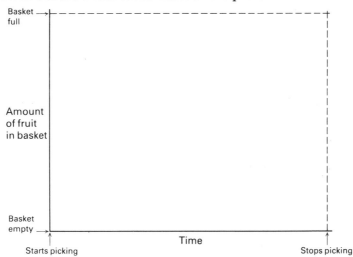

(b) If the lines $a$ and $b$ are continued, they will meet.
Calculate the angle at the point where they meet.
Show your working.

M8 Sandra goes fruit picking. This is something she has never done before.

At first she picks slowly.
Then she gets better at it until she is able to pick quite quickly.
Then she gets tired and picks more slowly until she stops when the basket is full.

Copy the axes below, and sketch a graph to show how the amount of fruit in Sandra's basket increases as she picks.

M9 Dress manufacturers use these formulas when they are designing clothes for 'average' women.

$$w = \frac{h}{2} - 20 \qquad s = \frac{w}{2} + 5$$

$h$ stands for the woman's height, in cm.
$w$ stand for the waist measurement, in cm.
$s$ stands for the shoulder measurement, in cm.

(a) What would be the waist measurement of a woman 170 cm tall?

(b) Calculate the waist and shoulder measurement of a woman who is 164 cm tall.

(c) Calculate the waist measurement of a woman whose shoulder measurement is 45 cm.

151

**M10** (a) Calculate the maximum volume of water which this tank can hold, in cubic metres. Do not round off your answer.

(b) Change the volume to litres. Give the result to the nearest litre.
($1\,\text{m}^3 = 1000$ litres.)

Maximum depth of water **0·76 m**

0·85 m          1·12 m

**M11**

Gillian and Robert each run a driving school.

During the last 12 months, 317 of Gillian's learner drivers took their driving test for the first time. 132 of them passed.

During the same period, 422 of Robert's learner drivers took their test for the first time. 189 of them passed.

Which driving school has the better record of first-time passes?
**Show clearly how you get your answer.**

**M12** Work out $\dfrac{43\cdot76 \times 0\cdot0163}{\sqrt{283\cdot71}}$ .

(a) Write down all the figures in your calculator display.

(b) Write your answer to 3 significant figures.

**M13** The speed of light in space is 299 800 000 m/s, to 4 significant figures.

Write this number in standard index form.

**M14** Find the value of $x$ if $\dfrac{450}{x} = 15$.

**M15** Which of these is the smallest?

(a) $2^{16}$   (b) $4^8$   (c) $8^4$   (d) $16^2$

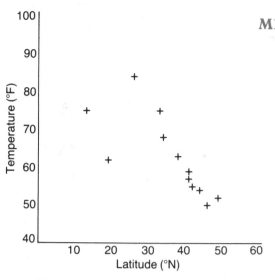

Temperature (°F)

Latitude (°N)

**M16** The maximum temperature in degrees Fahrenheit (°F) is recorded on a November day in twelve places in North America.

These temperatures are marked on this scatter diagram, together with the latitude of each place.

(The latitude, measured in degrees, tells you how far north a place is from the equator.)

What can you say about the relationship between latitude and temperature?

**M17** A 'penny farthing' bicycle has wheels of two different sizes.

Their diameters are 125 cm and 39·5 cm.

(a) Calculate the circumference of
 (i) the large wheel  (ii) the small wheel

(b) How far does the cycle travel as the large wheel makes 20 revolutions? Give your answer in **metres**.

(c) How many revolutions does the small wheel make in travelling the same distance?

**M18** A piston fits tightly in a vertical cylinder, trapping the air below it.

When a weight $w$ kg is placed on the piston, the height of the piston above the base is $h$ m.

$h$ is inversely proportional to $w$.

(a) Sketch a graph of $(w, h)$ on axes like these.

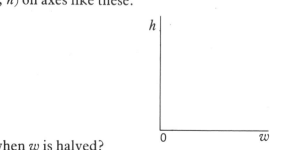

(b) What happens to $h$ when $w$ is halved?

(c) If $h = 45$ when $w = 250$, calculate $h$ when $w = 300$.

153

**M19** I travel to school by bus. Sometimes the bus arrives at the bus stop at the same time as I do. At other times I have to wait, for up to 10 minutes.

If the traffic lights are all green, the bus journey takes 7 minutes. Usually the journey takes longer, sometimes as long as 12 minutes.

It takes me 5 minutes to walk from home to the bus stop. It takes me 2 minutes to walk from the bus into school. I have to be in school by 8:45 a.m.

(a) By what time must I leave home to be **sure** of arriving at school on time?

(b) If I leave home at this time, what is the earliest I could arrive at school?

**M20** (a) Write down the sum of the interior angles of a quadrilateral.

(b) Draw this pentagon.
Draw a diagonal in it.

Work out the sum of the interior
angles of the pentagon.

(c) Suppose that two of the interior angles of a pentagon are each 120° and the other three angles are all equal to each other.
Work out the size of each of the other three angles.

**M21** This diagram shows a cross-section of a symmetrical railway embankment. It is in the shape of a trapezium.
The diagram is not to scale.

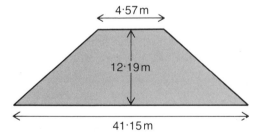

4·57 m

12·19 m

41·15 m

(a) (i) Calculate the area of the cross-section.

(ii) How many cubic metres of material are required to build a 100 m length of the embankment?

(b) This is a drawing of the
same cross-section.

(i) Calculate the length AB.

(ii) Calculate the angle θ.

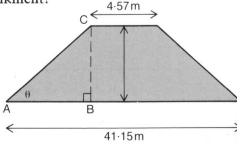

154

When measuring skid marks, the police can use this formula to estimate the speed of the vehicle.

$$s = \sqrt{(30fd)}$$

$s$ is the speed in miles per hour (m.p.h.)
$d$ is the length of the skid, in feet.
$f$ is a number which depends on the weather and the type of road.

This table shows some values of $f$.

| | | Road surface | |
|---|---|---|---|
| | | Concrete | Tar |
| **Weather** | Wet | 0·4 | 0·5 |
| | Dry | 0·8 | 1·0 |

(a) A car travelling on a wet concrete road makes a skid mark of length 80 feet. How fast was it travelling?

(b) (i) When the road surface is tar and the weather is dry, the formula may be written

$$s = \sqrt{(30d)}$$

Complete this table to show the values of $s$ for the given values of $d$, to 1 decimal place.

| $d$ | 50 | 100 | 150 | 200 | 250 |
|---|---|---|---|---|---|
| $30d$ | 1500 | | | | |
| $s = \sqrt{(30d)}$ | 38·7 | | | | |

    (ii) Draw axes, with $d$ from 0 to 250 (use 2 cm for 50) and $s$ from 0 to 100 (use 1 cm for 10).
Draw the graph of $(d, s)$.

    (iii) Use your graph to find how many feet a car would skid on a dry tar road at 75 m.p.h.

**M23** The frequency of a note played on the E-string of a violin
is **inversely** proportional to the length of
the vibrating part of the string.

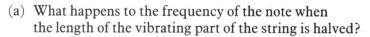

(a) What happens to the frequency of the note when
the length of the vibrating part of the string is halved?

(b) Frequency is measured in hertz (Hz).
When the vibrating length is 204 mm the frequency is 2048 Hz.
(i) Calculate the frequency when the length is 250 mm.
(ii) Calculate the length when the frequency is 3000 Hz.

**M24** In this question you will need the formula

Surface area of disc $= 2\pi r(r + t)$

where $r$ is the radius and $t$ the thickness.

The disease *multiple mycloma* causes
the red blood cells, which are like discs,
to stick together (like a pile of coins).

When the cells stick together, there are
fewer faces to absorb oxygen.

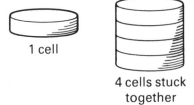

1 cell

4 cells stuck
together

The cells have a thickness of 2·2 microns
and a diameter of 7·2 microns.

The surface area is measured in
square microns.

(a) (i) What is the radius of a cell?

(ii) Find the surface area of one cell.

(iii) Find the total surface area
of four separate cells.

(b), (i) Find the surface area of four
cells stuck together.

(ii) Find the percentage decrease in surface area when four cells
stick together.